BEAUTIFUL BABY NAMES 2020

Find the perfect name
for your perfect baby

Lori Howarth

This book is dedicated to my loves,

Jason, Sonny & Sophie.
XXxx

Other Books by Lori Howarth

Global Baby Names, Celebrating Diversity

75,000+ Baby Names for the 21st Century

Beautiful Baby Names

House & Farm Names

Website

www.lorihowarth.com

Welcome to Beautiful Baby Names 2020

Beautiful Baby Names 2020 is a collection of the most beautiful baby names from around the world. Traditional names such as *Ruby, Isabelle, Grace, Rosemary, James, William, Charlie & Thomas* feature alongside a more exotic collection of beautiful names such as *Mirabella, Isabella, Valentina, Sol, Layla, Tennyson, Quenton* and *Stein*.

If you're not sure if a traditional boy or girl name will suit, then there is also a selection of unisex or names such as *Jett, Adair, Mackenzie, Aspen, Blake, Casey, Emerson, Logan, Ky, Milan* and *Zen*. Just look for the * next to a name/s.

For example:

*An

(Chinese) peace.

*Brooklyn

(Old English) pool by the stream.

Understanding the Name and Meaning

The layout of the names consists of the main stock name and one or more popular variations of the name followed by the origin/s in brackets and then the meaning. After the meaning may be more references to origin/s and further meanings in different languages. See below.

Arabella/Arabelle

(Latin/Italian) asked; beautiful altar; (Ger) eagle heroine.

Names that may have a unisex or gender-neutral spelling have an asterix * next to them. In some cases, some names alongside the unisex name do not have an asterix, this is because these names are traditionally used for a male or female name/s, depending on the section.

*Dion/Diona/Dione

(Greek) daughter of heaven and earth; Goddess of love.

*Mio

(Japanese) strength three times over.

Baby Names for 2020

Name trends over the past few decades have indicated that traditional names are the top picks for parents in countries such as Australia, New Zealand, United Kingdom, USA and Canada. This trend is expected to continue well into 2020 and beyond. The reason for this is simplicity and tradition. Parents are choosing names that have longevity, are easy to pronounce and easily recognised. Names with traditional spellings are preferred. For example, *Angelica* is preferred to a more unique spelling, *Angeliqua*. *Victoria* is preferred that *Vincentia*.

Names such as *Charlotte, Grace, Amelia, Olivia, Jack & William* are traditionally English names. Modern names have appeared in the list too, *Mia, Sienna & Aria*, for instance. The boy name section shows that most names on the list are very traditional with a mixture of English names & Hebrew or Bible names, *Benjamin, Samuel, Jacob & Isaac*.

However, never underestimate the effect of popular culture with names such as *Ziggy & Amabella* (Big Little Lies (2017) and *Bron, Ygritte, Gilly* and *Bran* from Game of Thrones (2011-2019).

Below are some names to consider for babies in 2020, including vintage, modern and gender-neutral names for consideration. The most popular names are from Australia, name predictions are from the UK, USA, New Zealand Australia. See the following list for popular names and name predictions.

Poplar Baby Names

The baby names listed below in alphabetical order, have been taken from all over the world to give the big picture of popular baby names in 2019 and to give you an idea of what the name trends are for 2020 and beyond. These countries include, Australia, USA, UK, Norway, Sweden, Philipines, China, Ireland, Scotland, African American, New Zealand, Russia, Italy, India, Hawaiian, Spain, Native American & Australian Aboriginal.

Global Popular Girl Names for 2019

Aaliyah, Abbey, Adah, Adalina, Adelita, Adhira, Adora, Ai, Ailani, Aileen, Aimee, Alanna, Aleksis, Aleta, Alexandra, Alexis, Alice, Alinta, Alisha, Alma, Althea, Amalie, Amanda, Amber, Amelia, Amihan, Amor, Amparo, An, Ana, Analyn, Angel, Anika, Aniyah, Anna, Annabelle, Anne, Annie, Antonia, Aoibhe, Aoife, Arabella, Aria, Ariadna, Ariana, Asmee, Aubrey, Audrey, Aurora, Ava, Avni, Bai, Bao, Basilia, Bella, Benita, Blessica, Bo, Bonita, Bonny, Brianna, Caitlin, Camilla, Caprice, Cara, Carina, Carmen, Catherine, Celestina, Celia, Chang, Charlie, Charlotte, Chaska, Chen, Chenoa, Cheyenne, Chloe, Chu, Chumani, Ciara, Clara, Cora, Cree, Daisy, Dakota, Dalisay, Dana, Danica, Danya, Darcey, Destiny, Diamond, Dolores, Dyani, Ebba, Eilidh, Eliza, Elizabeth, Ella, Ellie, Elsie, Emilia, Emily, Emma, Erin, Esme, Eva, Evelyn, Everleigh, Evie, Faye, Felicity, Florence, Floribeth, Freya, Frida, Georgia, Gia, Giada, Gigi, Grace, Hadley, Hai, Halle, Halona, Hannah, Harper, Harriet, Hazel, Heidi, Hollie, Holly, Hope, Huan, Iluka, Imani, Imogen, Ingrid, Iona, Isabella, Isabelle, Ishana, Isla, Isobel, Ivy, Jada, Jaslene, Jasmine, Jean, Jedda, Jessica, Jia, Jiao, Jing, Jordan, Kachina, Kaia, Kaiah, Kailani, Kala, Kalena, Kalia, Kalinda, Karri, Katie, Kayla, Kayleigh, Keilani, Kennedy, Keya, Kiara, Kim, Kima, Kimana, Kimaya, Kiona, Koko, Krisha, Kylie, Lacey, Lai, Laila, Lailani, Larissa, Lauren, Layla, Lee, Lei, Leigh, Leilani, Leotie, Li, Lian, Liezel, Lila, Lilibeth, Lin, Lily, Lin Linnéa, Lola, Lottie, Lu'lu`, Lucy, Luna, Mackenzie, Madison, Maeve, Mahalia, Mahika, Maisie, Maja, Malaya, Maliya, Mara, Marcella, Margaret, Marie, Marisol, Mary, Matilda, Maya, Megan, Mei, Mey, Mia, Mila, Milan, Milani, Milly, Ming, Mireia, Mishka, Molly, Montana, Mya, Myla, Naitee, Nalani, ancy, Natalia, Nenita, Neysa, Niall, Niamh, Ning, Nioka, Nora, Olivia, Oliwia, Onowa, Paige, Pavati, Penelope, Perla, Petunia, Phoebe, Pia, Piper, Poppy, Prisha, Qi, Qiao, Qiu, Quinn, Rachel, Raphaela, Rebecca, Reign, Reyna, Rhiannon, Rita, Rosamie, Rose, Rosie, Rosilita, Ruby, Rubylyn, Ruth, Ryka, Saanvi, Sahalie, Salali, Sanchia, Sara, Sarah, Savannah, Scarlett, Selma, Sens, Shanaya, Shania, Shannon, Shanoah, Shi, Shu, Sienna, Siobhain, Sofia, Sol, Song, Sophia, Sophie, Summer, Susanita, Tai, Tala, Talia, Tama, Tamryn, Tanvi, Tara, Taylor, Teofila, Tiana, Tona, Tove, Trini, Trinity, Valentia, Vanna, Vera, Veronica, Victoria, Violet, Violetta, Viti, Wei, Willow, Xenia, Xia, Xiomara, Yan, Yin, Ynes, Zan, Zara, Zarita, Zheng, Zhi, Zhora, Zhu, Zoe.

Girl Name Predictions for 2020

Abbey, Abigail, Adelaide, Agnes, Ailani, Alice, Alicia, Alison, Alma, Alva, Amelia, Amelie, Anastasia, Anika, Annabel, Annabelle, Annie, Antonella, Antonia, April, Arabella, Aria, Ariana, Arya, Astrid, Aubree, Aubrey, Audrey, Aura, Aurora, Ava, Avalon, Beatrix, Bella, Bellamy, Belle, Bianca, Bo, Bonnie, Bonny, Bree, Bria, Brianna, Briar, Briella, Brielle, Caitlin, Calliope, Camille, Carina, Catriona, Celine, Charlie, Charlotte, Chu, Ciara, Claire, Clara, Clementine, Cleo, Cornelia, Daisy, Darcey, Edith, Elenore, Eliana, Elise, Ella, Elle, Ellie, Elsa, Elsie, Elvira, Emelie, Emilia, Ester, Euganie, Eva, Evelyn, Everlee, Everleigh, Evie, Filippa, Filomena, Flora, Florence, Frankie, Freja, Freya, Genevieve, Gia, Gigi, Grace, Gracie, Gracelyn, Greer, Greta, Gretal, Haisley, Halona, Hanna, Harper, Heidi, Hilda, Hollie, Holly, Hope, Ida, Iluka, Imogen, Indigo, Ines, Inga, Ingrid, Innes, Iona, Ireland, Iris, Isabel, Isabell, Isabella, Isabelle, Isla, Isobel, Ivy, Jane, Jasmine, Jessica, Julia, Juni, Kaia, Kate, Katie, Keiley, Kiara, Kiona, Koko, Laila, Lane, Lani, Laroux, Layla, Leah, Leia, Leila, Lexi, Lian, Linnéa, Liv, Livia, Lo, Lola, Lottie, Lovisa, Lucia, Lucie, Lucy, Lykke, Lyra, Madeleine, Mae, Maeve, Maisie, Maja, Majken, Margaux, Maria, Marie, Marigold, Marisol, Marta, Maryam, Matilda, May, Maya, Megan, Meghan, Mei, Meja, Melanie, Melissa, Mia, Mila, Milan, Milani, Millicent, Milly, Mira, Miranda, Miria, Mishka, Moa, Mollie, Molly, Mya, Myla, Nalani, Natalia, Nellie, Niamh, Nioka, Nora, Nova, Olivia, Opal, Paisley, Pearl, Pearle, Penelope, Penny, Philomena, Phoebe, Pia, Piper, Poppy, Posie, Primrose, Qi, Raven, Reyna, Rhiannon, Ronja, Rosalee, Rosamie, Rosie, Roxy, Ruby, Ryka, Saanvi, Sahalie, Sallie, Sally, Saoirse, Sara, Scarlett, Selene, Serena, Shanaya, Shania, Shannon, Shu, Sia, Sibella, Sienna, Signe, Sigrid, Sirir, Sofia, Sofie, Sophia, Sophie, Stella, Stina, Summer, Sunnie, Sunny, Svea, Sydney, Tai, Talia, Tamryn, Tai, Talia, Tamryn, Tara, Tatiana, Thea, Tia, Tiana, Tiara, Tilde, Tuva, Tully, Valentina, Velvet, Vera, Veronica, Violet, Violeta, Violetta, Willow, Wima, Winter, Zara, Zaria, Zoey, Zoey.

Popular Boy Names for 2019

Aaron, Adam, Aiden, Akanksh, Áke, Alan, Alarico, Albie, Albin, Alejo, Alek, Alessandro, Alexander, Alfie, Alo, Amador, Amari, Amidio, An, Andres, Angus, Anthony, Archie, Arlo, Armando, Arthur, Atticus, Avery, Ayaan, Bai, Bane, Basilio, Benedicto, Benito, Benjamin, Bo, Bobby, Branson, Bryson, Calian, Callum, Cameron, Carlos, Carter, Cayo, Celino, Chao, Charles, Charlie, Chase, Chaska, Shayton, Chen, Chesmu, Chi, Chris, Christian, Christopher, Chung, Clemente, Conor, Cooper, Dakari, Dakota, Dan, Daniel, Dario, Dasan, Dasya, David, Dean, Deangelo, Demetrio, Desiderio, Diego, Dimitrios, Domingo, Donte, Dyami, Dylan, Edmundo, Edward, Elan, Eli, Elias, Elijah, Elsu, Emil, Enrique, Eoghan, Eoin, Ethan, Evan, Felix, Feng, Fernan, Fernando, Filip, Finlay, Finley, Finn, Florencio, Frankie, Freddie, George, Gian, Gilberto, Gino, Giorgio, Giovanni, Grayson, Hai, Hako, Hakon, Harley, Harris, Harrison, Harry, Henry, Heratio, Hernando, Hong, Hotah, Hua, Hudson, Hugh, Humberto, Hunter, Iago, Ian, Injgo, Isaac, Isaiah, Isak, Isandro, Jack, Jacob, Jacy, Jai, Jake, James, Jamie, Japa, Jarli, Jash, Jasper, Jaxon, Jay, Jenaro, Jenson, Jesus, Jia, Jiemba, Joaquin, John, Jordan, Joseph, Josiah, Juan, Jude, Jun, Kabir, Kai, Kainoa, Kale, Kaleo, Keanu, Kekoa, Kele, Kian, Knoton, Koa, Kohana, Koi, Kyle, Lachlan, Laksh, Landon, Lashawn, Lei, Leo, Leon, Leonardo, Leoncio, Levi, Lewis, Li, Liam, Liang, Lincoln, Lochie, Logan, Lok, Lorcan, Lorenzo, Louis, Luca, Luis, Lukas, Lyle, Macario, Mahkah, Maks, Makya, Malik, Manan, Manuel, Marcio, Mario, Mark, Mason, Matteo, Matto, Max, Maximiano, Maximo, Michael, Miguel, Miro, Mohammad, Montana, Montrell, Muhammad, Naksh, Natalio, Natanael, Nathan, Nathaniel, Niall, Nic, Nico, Nimit, Ning, Noah, Oisin, Oliver, Ollie, Oran, Oscar, Oskar, Patricio, Patrick, Paytah, Petrov, Powa, Qi, Qiao, Qiu, Raini, Raj, Ramiro, Ranbir, Reggie, Rhys, Riley, Rishaan, Robbie, Robby, Robert, Rocco, Romeo, Rory, Ross, Rowan, Rudra, Ryan, Sadhil, Sahale, Samoset, Samuel, Sawyer, Scott, Sean, Sebaastian, Shan, Shane, Shaun, Shawn, Shawree, Shen, Shilah, Shui, Silas, Sixten, Sonny, Stefano, Stephen, Steven, Struan, Sying, Tadgh, Taj, Taksh, Tala, Tamas, Tao, Taos, Tarka, Tatanka, Theo, Theodore, Thomas, Toby, Tom, Tommy, Ved, Victor, Vittorio, Wang, Wei, Wen, William, Wyatt, Xavier, Yash, Zac, Zack, Zare, Zak, Zory, Zuber.

Boy Name Predictions for 2020

Adam, Aiden, Albie, Alejo, Alek, Alessandro, Alex, Alexander, Alfie, Amari, Andres, Angus, Antonio, Archer, Archie, Arlo, Ash, Ashton, Austin, Axel, Beau, Ben, Benny, Benjamin, Bjorn, Blake, Bodie, Bowie, Bran, Branson, Brodie, Brooklyn, Calian, Carter, Cash, Cayo, Charles, Charlie, Chase, Chen, Chi, Cillian, Clay, Clayton, Clint, Clyde, Cole, Colt, Conor, Cooper, Damon, Dan, Daniel, Danny, Dante, Darcy, David, Deangelo, Declan, Delano, Denver, Desiderio, Dex, Diego, Dylan, Eduardo, Edward, Edwin, Elan, Eli, Eoin, Ethan, Evan, Ezra, Felix, Fernando, Filip, Finlay, Finley, Finn, Fionn, Florencio, Flynn, Frankie, Freddie, Gabriel, George, Gian, Gino, Giovanni, Grayson, Gus, Harley, Harris, Harry, Harvey, Hawk, Hayden, Henry, Heratio, Hermando, Hudson, Hugh, Hugo, Hunter, Huxley, Iago, Isaac, Isaiah, Jack, Jackson, Jacob, Jacy, Jagger, Jai, James, Jamie, Jason, Jasper, Jaxon, Jay, Jenson, Jia, Joaquin, Joey, Johnny, Joshua, Josiah, Juan, Kai, Kainoa, Kale, Kekoa, Kele, Kenrick, Kenzo, Kian, Kingston, Knight, Koi, Ky, Kyle, Lachlan, Landon, Lane, Layton, Lee, lei, Lennon, Leo, Leon, Leonardo, Leroy, Levi, Lewis, Lex, Li, Liam, Lincoln, Lochie, Lochlan, Logan, Lorcan, Lorenzo, Louis, Luca, Lucas, Luka, Luke,

Lyle, Macario, Makya, Malik, Marcio, Marlon, Mason, Mateo, Matteo, Matthew, Maurice, Max, Maximo, Maximus, Maxwell, Memphis, Mercer, Mick, Milan, Milo, Montrell, Murray, Nash, Nashville, Natalio, Natanael, Nate, Nathaniel, Nic, Nico, Nik, Niko, Noah, Oliver, Ollie, Oscar, Oskar, Owen, Patricio, Patrick, Qi, Qiao, Raini, Ralph, Ramiro, Raphael, Reggie, Reuben, River, Robert, Robbie, Rocco, Roman, Romeo, Ronnie, Rory, Rudy, Ryan, Salvadore, Samuel, Sawyer, Scott, Sean, Sebastian, Shae, Shaun, Shawn, Shay, Silas, Sonny, Soren, Spencer, Stefano, Stephen, Steven, Tadhg, Tate, Tennyson, Theodore, Thom, Thomas, Tim, Timmy, Timothy, Tom, Tommy, Torin, Valentino, Van, Victor, Vincent, Vittorio, Will, William, Wyatt, Xavier, Zac, Zack, Zak, Zane, Zayne, Zory.

Popular Gender-Neutral Baby Names

Acton, Addison, Ainsley, Ajay, Alex, Ali, Angel, Arden, Ashley, Ashton, Bailey, Billy, Brook, Cary, Casey, Cassidy, Charlie, Cody, Corey, Dakota, Dale, Dallon, Dallas, Dana, Danyon, Darcy, Deven, Devon, Drew, Dylan, Eden, Finley, Frankie, Harley, Harper, Hurley, Jamie, Jessie, Jody, Jordan, Jules, Kelly, Kennedy, Lane, Lee, Lennon, Logan, Mackenzie, Morgan, Oakley, Peyton, Phoenix, Piper, Quinn, Reese, Ricky, Riley, River, Rowan, Skyler, Sydney, Taylor, Valentine, Yardley.

Name Predictions Gender-Neutral Names

Addison, Adrian, Aiden, Ainsley, Airlie, Ajay, Alex, Ali, Amory, Andie, Andy, Angel, Arden, Ari, Ash, Ashley, Ashton, Aspen, Austin, Avery, Bailey, Billy, Blaine, Blaise, Blaize, Blake, Blayse, Blayze, Bobby, Bodhi, Braxton, Brent, Brett, Britt, Brodie, Brook, Cal, Cales, Cam, Cameron, Campbell, Carey, Carson, Cary, Cassidy, Cheyne, Chi, Chris, Christian, Coby, Cody, Colorado, Corey, Cory, Dakota, Dale, Dallan, Dallas, Dana, Danny, Darcy, Daryl, Deven, Devlin, Devon, Dillon, Dion, Dorian, Drew, Dylan, Eddie, Eddy, Eden, Ellery, Ellington, Ellison, Emerson, Emery, Erin, Evan, Everlee, Everley, Fallon, Finlay, Finley, Frankie, Gabriel, Gene, Georgie, Gray, Grayson, Grey, Greyson, Hailey, Harley, Harlow, Harper, Haven, Hayden, Hunter, Huntley, Hurley, Huxley, India, Indiana, Jacky, Jacoba, Jade, Jae, Jai, Jaiden, Jaime, Jak, Jalen, James, Jamie, Jan, Jay, Jazz, Jean, Jess, Jesse, Jessie, Jo, Joey, Jonny, Jordan, Joss, Jules, Julian, Kade, Kaden, Kai, Kale, Kassidy, Keeley, Kelly, Kelsey, Kendal, Kendell, Kenji, Kennedy, Kenzie, Kia, Kieren, Kingsley, Kingston, Kris, Ky, Kyan, Kyle, Lake, Lane, Laurie, Leah, Leander, Lee, Leigh, Leighton, Lennon, Lennox, Linden, Linton, Lochie, Logan, London, Lonny, Lou, Loxley, Lucky, Mackenzie, Madison, Marlow, Marty, Mason, Mattie, Micky, Misha, Monroe, Montana, Morgan, Morry, Neo, Nevada, Nic, Nick, Nicky, Niko, Oakley, Paris, Parker, Pat, Perry, Peta, Peyton, Phoenix, Piper, Presley, Quinn, Rain, Ray, Rayne, Reagan, Reece, Reed, Reese, Regan, Remi, Rene, Rhett, Ricky, Riley, Rio, River, Roan, Robin, Robyn, Rory, Roux, Rowan, Rudy, Ryan, Rylan, Sacha, Sage, Sal, Sam, Sammie, Sammy, Sandy, Sasha, Sawyer, Scout, Sean, Shae, Shay, Shiloh, Sky, Skye, Skylar, Skyler, Slade, Sloan, Sloane, Stevi, Stevie, Storm, Stormy, Sunny, Sydney, Tailor, Taj, Tanner, Tatum, Taylor, Teddy, Tempest, Thai, Tobie, Toby, Toni, Tony, Tristan, Tully, Tyler, Val, Vale, Valentine, Vic, Vik, Whitney, Wren, Yardley, Zaiden, Zane, Zion.

Abbreviations

Beautiful Baby Names have been collected from around the world and includes languages such as: Native American, New Zealand Māori, Nordic, Old English, Chinese, Japanese, German, French, Australian Aboriginal, Irish, Scottish and so much more. Below shows the abbreviation of the cultural name and the full language.

(Abor) Australian Aboriginal
(Afr) African
(Algon) Algonquin
(Amer) American
Anglo (Anglo Saxon)
(Arab) Arabic
(Ara) Aramaic
(Arm) Armenian
(Austral) Australian
(Basq) Basque
(Blkft) Blackfoot
(Bret) Breton
(Bulg) Bulgarian
(Bur) Burmese
(Cam) Cambodian
(Chero) Cherokee
(Chey) Cheyenne
(Chin) Chinese
(Chip) Chippewa
(Com) Comanche
(Crk) Creek
(Dan) Danish
(Dut) Dutch
(Egypt) Egyptian
(Eng) English
(Fij) Fijian
(Fin) Finnish
(Gae) Gaelic
(Ghan) Ghanaian
(Goth) Gothic
(Grk) Greek
(Gyp) Gypsy

(Haus) Hausa
(Haw) Hawaiian
(Heb) Hebrew
(Hin) Hindi
(Hop) Hopi
(Hung) Hungarian
(Ice) Icelandic
(Indo) Indonesian
(Ir) Irish
(Isra) Israeli
(Ital) Italian
(Jap) Japanese
(Kaur) Kaurna
(Kor) Korean
(Lak) Lakota
(Lat) Latin
(Lith) Lithuanian
(Māori) New Zealand Māori
(M/Eng) Middle English
(Mi) Miwok
(Moq) Moquelumnan
(Mw) Mwera
(Nat/Amer) Native American
(Neth) Netherlands
(Nez) Nez Perce
(Nrs) Norse
(Nav) Navajo
(Nig) Nigerian
(Nor) Norwegian
(O/Eng) Old English
(O/Fren) Old French
(O/Ger) Old German

(O/Nrs) Old Norse
(O/Span) Old Spanish
(O/Wel) Old Welsh
(Os) Osage
(Pak) Pakistani
(Per) Persian
(Phoen) Phoenician
(Pol) Polish
(Poly) Polynesian
(Pon) Ponca
(Port) Portuguese
(Pun) Punjabi
(Run) Runyankore
(Russ) Russian
(Sans) Sanskrit
(Scan) Scandinavian
(Scot) Scottish
(Sio) Sioux
(Slav) Slavic
(Span) Spanish
(Swah) Swahili
(Swed) Swedish
(Thai) Thai
(Tib) Tibetan
(Tong) Tongan
(Turk) Turkish
(Viet) Vietnamese
(Wata) Watamare
(Wel) Welsh
(Wem) Wemba-Wemba

(Wir) Wiradjuri   (Yid) Yiddish   (Yor) Yoruba

Girl Names

A

Abbey
(Hebrew) high father. A feminine
short form of Abraham.

Abigail
(Hebrew) born of a joyous father.
A combination of Abby and Gail.

Abriana/Abriane
(Italian) mother of the multitudes.
A feminine form of Abraham.

Abriella/Abrielle
(Hebrew/Italian) strength of God. A
form of Gabrielle or Brielle.

Ada/Adah
(Hebrew) ornament; crowned; (Eng)
prosperous; (Lat) noble birth.

Adela
(German/Spanish) noble. A short
form of Adelaide.

Adelaide
(German) noble, cheerful and kind.

Adelina/Adeline
(German) noble; serpent.

Adell/Adella/Adelle
(German) noble, cheerful and kind.
A short form of Adelaide.

Adena
(Hebrew) sensuous; delicate;
(Grk) noble; delicate.

Adina
(Aboriginal) good; (Heb)

voluptuous, beautiful.

Adriana/Adriane
(Greek) dark-complexioned;
dark-haired.

Aerona
(Welsh) berry.

Afina
(Hebrew) young deer.

*Afton
(Old English) from Afton in England.

Aida
(Hebrew) ornament; crowned;
(Eng) prosperous; (Lat) noble
birth; (O/Fren) assistant. The
Italian form of Ada.

*Aidan
(Irish) small and fiery.

Ailsa
(German) happy.

*Aine
(Scottish) belonging to oneself;
(Ir) joy; fire. A short form of names
beginning with 'Ain' e.g. Ainsley.

*Ainsley
(Scottish) open country meadow;
strong and courageous meadow;
(O/Eng) meadow clearing.

Aiofe
(Irish) beautiful and radiant;
happiness.

Airlea
(Old English) airy meadow; light-
filled meadow.

Airleas
(Irish) promise.

Aislin/Aislinn/Aissa
(Scottish) dream.

Aiyana
(Hindi) innocent. A form of
Ayanna.

Alaina/*Alaine/Alana
(Irish) harmony; peace; fair and beautiful; bright and cheerful. A form of Alanna and a feminine form of Alan.

Alamea
(Hawaiian) precious.

Alani
(Hawaiian) orange tree.

Alanis
(Irish/Scottish) beautiful and bright child.

Alanna/Alannah/Alana
(Irish/Scottish) harmony; peace; fair and beautiful; bright and cheerful. A form of Alanna and a feminine form of Alan.

Alastrina
(Greek/Scottish) avenger. The feminine form of Alastair.

*Alate
(Spanish) truthful.

Aleah
(Hebrew) lion-like; (O/Eng) a meadow.

Aleene
(Greek/Dutch) alone; light bringer; light. A form of Aileen.

Aleka
(Hawaiian/German) noble; (Grk) truth; defender or humankind. A form of Allison or Alex.

Alena
(Greek/Latin/Russian) light bringer; light. A form of Helen/Aileen.

Aleria
(Latin) eagle.

Alesia
(Greek) helper.

Aleta
(Latin) winged; (Grk) wanderer.

***Alex/Alexa/Alexandra/
Alexandria/Alexia**
(Greek) defender of humankind. A feminine form of Alexander.

Alexis
(Greek) good and kind.

*Ali
(Greek) truth. A short form of names starting with 'Ali' e.g. Alison.

Alice
(Greek) truth; (O/Ger) noble. A form of Alison.

Alicia
(Greek) truth.

Alida
(Greek) beautifully clothed; (Lat) little wing.

Alina
(Slavic) bright and beautiful; (Ir) harmonious and fair.

Alisa/Alyssa
(Hebrew) joy.

Alison/Allison
(Greek) truth; (O/Ger) noble.

Aliza
(Hebrew/Spanish) joy; oath to God. A form of Eliza/Elizabeth.

Allegra
(Latin) cheerful; (Ital) lively.

Allira
(Aboriginal) quartz stone.

Allison/Allyson
(Greek) truth; (O/Ger) noble;

(O/Eng) Alice's child; Ally's child.

A form of Alice.

Ally/Allie
(Greek) truth; (O/Ger) noble.

Alma
(Arabic) learned; (Lat) nourishing
support; (Span/Ital) spirit; (Heb)
young woman.

Almeda/Ameta
(Welsh) shapely; (Lat) ambitious.

Almira
(Arabic) princess; truth; (Eng)
noble and famous. A feminine
form of Elmer.

Almita
(Latin) kind.

Alodie
(Old English) wealthy.

Aloha
(Hawaiian) greetings or
farewell.

Alona
(English/Latin) solitary.

Aloysia
(German) famous, glorious warrior
of battle. A feminine form of
Aloysius.

Alva
(Spanish/Latin) white.

Alyssa
(Greek) sensible; yellow flower;
(Heb) joy.

*Amar
(Cherokee) water; (Afr/Fren) born
on a Saturday.

Amabel/Amabelle
(Latin) lovable beauty; (Ir) joy; queen

of the fairies.

*Amal
(Arabic) hope.

Amalea/Amalia
(German) hard working; (Heb) labour
of God. A form of Amelia.

Amaline
(German) hard working;
flatterer (Lat/Fren). A form
of Emmaline.

Amara
(Greek) eternal beauty.

Amarina
(Aboriginal) rain.

Amarinda
(Greek) longevity.

Amaris
(Hebrew) promise of God.

Amaryllis
(Greek) fresh stream.

Amaya
(Japanese) raining at night.
Ambel/Ambelle/Amabelle
(Latin) beloved and beautiful.

Amber
(Egyptian) light; (O/Fren) the
amber jewel; (Arab) jewel;
(Scot) fierce; fossilized tree resin;
(Chin) soul of a tiger.

Amberlie
(Old French) the amber jewel;
(Egypt) light; (Arab) jewel;
(Scot) fierce.

Ambrosia
(Polish/Greek) divine immortal. A
feminine form of Ambrose.

Amelia/Emilia

(German) hard working; (Heb) labour
of God.

Amelinda
(Latin/Spanish) beloved and pretty.

Amethyst
(Greek) beneficent; a purple-
coloured gem.

Amiel
(German) hard working; (Heb) the
people of God; God is with me.

Amira
(Arabic) princess.

Amita
(Hebrew) truth.

Amity
(Latin) friend.

Amorette
(Latin/English) beloved and
little.

Amorita
(Latin) beloved.

Amy/Ami/Amie/
Ame/Amee
(Latin) beloved friend; (Fren) love.

*An
(Chinese) peace.

Ana
(Hebrew/Hawaiian/Spanish) graceful.
A form of Hannah/Anna.

Anaïs/Anais
(Hebrew) graceful. A form of Ann.

Anastasia
(Greek/Spanish/Russian) resurrection;
springtime.

*Ancelin/Ancelina/Anceline
(Latin) land; the knight's spear

attendant. The feminine form
of Lancelot.

*Andra
(Old Norse) breath.

Andrea/Andria
(Latin/Greek) strong and courageous.
A feminine form of Andre/Andrew.

Andriana/Andrianna
(Latin) strong and courageous. A
feminine form of Andrew.

Aneira
(Welsh) honourable.

Aneko
(Japanese) eldest sister.

*Angel
(Greek) messenger of God;
angel. A short form of Angela/
Angelique.

Angelica
(Greek) messenger of God;
angel-like.

Angelina
(Greek/Russian) messenger of
God; angel. A Russian form
of Angelica.

Angelique
(Greek/French) messenger of
God; angel.

Anh
(Vietnamese) flower.

Ani
(Hawaiian) beautiful.

Ania
(Polish/Hebrew) graceful. A
form of Anna/Hannah.

Aniela
(Hebrew) graceful. The Polish
form of Anna.

Anika
(Scandinavian/Hebrew) graceful.
A form of Ann.

Anita
(Hebrew) graceful. A form of
Ann/Anna.

Anja
(Russian) graceful. A form of Anne.

Ann/Anna/Anne/Annie
(Hebrew) graceful. A short form
of names starting with 'Ann'
e.g. Annelise.

Anna
(Arapaho) mother; (Heb) graceful.
A form of Ann/e.

Annabell/Annabella/Annabelle
(Hebrew/Latin/Italian/French)
Pure and beautiful.

Anneka
(Hebrew) graceful. The Dutch and
Swedish form of Anna.

Annelise
(Hebrew/German) graceful
satisfaction.

Annetta/Annette
(Hebrew/French/Old English) little
and graceful. A form of Anne.

Annilie
(Finnish) graceful. A form of Ana
or Anna.

Annina
(Hebrew) graceful.

Annmarie
(Hebrew) graceful sea of bitterness;
graceful lady of the sea. A
combination of Ann and Marie.

Annona
(Greek) Roman Goddess of the

yearly crop.

Annora
(Greek) light; (Lat) honour. The Old English
form of Eleanor and Helen.

Anselma
(Old Norse/Old German) warrior
with divine protection. A feminine
form of Anselm.

***Anstice**
(Greek) resurrection. An English
form of Anastasia.

Anthea
(Greek) flower.

Antoinette
(Latin/French) priceless. A feminine
form of Anthony.

Antonia
(Latin) priceless. A feminine form of
Anthony.

Anya
(Hebrew/Russian) graceful. The
Russian form of Anna.

Aolani
(Hawaiian) heavenly cloud.

Aphrodite
(Greek) Goddess of love.

Appollonia
(Greek) sunlight. A feminine form
of Apollo.

April
(Latin) open; born in the
month of April.

Ara
(Arabic) rain maker; (Grk)
altar; Goddess of vengeance

and destruction.

Arabella/Arabelle

(Latin/Italian) asked; beautiful
altar; (Ger) eagle heroine.

Ardeen/Ardeena
(Latin) glowing.

Ardelia
(Latin/Greek) visibly glowing.
A combination of Ara and
Delia.

*Arden
(Old English) glowing valley.

Areta
(Greek) excellent.

*Aria
(Italian) operatic song.

Ariana
(Latin/Hebrew) holy and graceful
believer.

Arianwen
(Welsh) silver/white haired friend;
(Lat/Wel) silver or white-haired
believer.

Ariel/Ariella/Arielle
(Hebrew) God's lion; light
of God.

Arietta/Ariette
(Latin/Italian/Old English) little
melody.

*Arya
(Italian) operatic song.

*Ash
(Old English) ash tree.

*Asha
(Persian) truth; (Swah) life.

Ashanti
(Swahili) west; (Afr) a tribal name.

Ashaylin
(Old English) ash tree fairy by
the stream.

Ashia
(Arabic) life. A form of Aisha.

Ashira
(Hebrew) wealthy.

Ashlea/Ashlee/*Ashley
(Old English) ash tree meadow.

*Ashling
(Irish) dreamer; visionary;

(O/Eng) young ash tree.

*Asia
(Swahili) life; (Eng) sunrise
in the east.

*Aspen
(English) the aspen tree.

*Asperity
(English) sharp tempered.

*Asta/*Aster/Astera/
Asteria/Astra/Astria
(Greek) star.

Astrid
(Old Norse) divine strength;
(Grk) star.

Atalaya
(Spanish) guardian; (Arab) watch
tower.

Atara
(Hebrew) crown.

Athalia/Athalie
(Hebrew) God is praised highly.

Athena
(Greek) wisdom; the Greek
Goddess of wisdom.

Auberte
(French) noble; industrious;
bright; famous. A feminine
form of Albert.

Aubree/*Aubrey
(Old French) reddish/brown-haired
ruler; powerful and wise ruler;
elf; (Ger) bear; noble.

Aubrianne
(Old French/Hebrew) reddish/
brown-haired, graceful ruler;
elf; (Ir/Eng) graceful and
strong one with fair hair.

Audrey
(Old English) noble strength.

Audris
(German) wealthy and fortunate.

Augusta
(Latin) majestic; royal one worthy
of honour; born in August. A feminine
form of Augustus.

*Austin/Austine/Austina
(Latin) little but majestic; royal one

worthy of honour; born in August.
A feminine form of Austin.

Autumn
(Latin) autumn; born in autumn;
fall.

Ava
(Greek) eagle; (Lat) bird-like.

*Avalon
(Latin) island.

Avara
(Sanskrit) the youngest child.

Aveline/Avelina
(German/French) hazelnut.

Avena
(Latin) oats.

Avera
(Hebrew) one who goes
beyond.

*Averil/Averila
(Latin) open; born in the month
of April; (Ger/Old/Eng)
boar battle.

*Avery
(Old French) confirmation.

Aviva
(Hebrew) anew; springtime.

*Avoca
(Ir) sweet valley.

*Avril
(Old English) born in April;
(Lat) open; boar warrior. The
French form of April.

*Awena
(Welsh) poetry.

Aya
(Hebrew) swift bird.

Ayanna
(Hindi) innocent.

Ayla
(Hebrew) oak tree.

Azalea
(Old English) flower; (Grk)
dry earth.

Azura/*Azure

(Persian) blue lapis stone;
(Fren/Eng) sky blue.

B

*Bailey
(Old French) bailiff or sheriff's
officer; one who pours water from
the meadow.

Basia
(Hebrew) God's daughter.

Basilla
(Greek) majestic; the basil herb. A
feminine form of Basil.

Beatrice
(Latin) she brings happiness.

Bel
(Hindi) apple tree in the sacred wood;
(Fren) beautiful. A short form of names
starting with 'Bel' e.g. Belinda.

Bela/Bella/Belda
(Italian) beautiful; (Hun) bright one;
(Slav) white.

Belica
(Spanish) dedication to God.

Bella/Belle
(Italian) beautiful; dedicated to God.
A short form of names ending in
'bella' e.g. Isabella/Arabella.

Benecia/Benedicta

(Latin) blessed. A feminine
form of Benedict.

Beth
(Hebrew) from the house of God; oath

to God; (Ir) life. A short form of names
starting with or containing 'Beth' e.g.
Elizabeth/Bethany.

Bethann
(Hebrew) from the house of
God's grace. A combination of Beth
and Ann or a form of Bethany.

Bethany
(Aramaic) from the house of affliction;
the house of song; (Heb) from the
house of God's grace. A
combination of Beth and
Ann/Annie.

*Bevin
(Irish) sweetly singing.

Bian
(Vietnamese) secret.

Bianca
(Italian) white.

Bina
(Swahili) dancer.

*Blaine
(Irish) thin; (O/Eng) flame.

*Blair
(Irish) marsh plain; (Scot) field of
battle.

*Blaise
(English) burning flames; (Lat)
sprouting.

*Blake
(Old English) dark-haired;
dark-complexioned; black.

Blanca
(Spanish) white.

*Bo
(Old Norse) house owner; (Chin)
precious; (Eng/Fren) beautiful. A
form of Beau.

Boann
(Irish) white cow; (Eng/
Hebrew) white grace.

Bona
(Latin) good. A feminine form
of Bono.

Bonita
(Spanish) pretty and little.

Bonny
(Scottish) pretty and good;
(Ir) pretty and charming.

Breana/Breanna/Breanne
(Irish/Old English) strong and
gracious victory. A combination
of Bree and Anna/Anne.

Bree
(Irish) strong victory. A short
form of names staring with 'Bree'
e.g. Breena.

Breena
(Irish) fairy palace.

Brenna
(Irish/Scottish) little raven;
black-haired.

Bretta
(Irish/Scottish) from Britain. A
feminine form of Brett.

Bria
(Scottish) hill; (Ir) strong and
honourable. A feminine form
of Brian.

Brianna/Brianne

(Irish/Old English/Hebrew) strong
and graceful hill; (Ir) strong, graceful
and honourable. A feminine
form of Brian.

*Briar
(Old English) wild rose.

Bridey
(Irish) strength; (Eng) little bride.
A form of Bridget.

Bridget
(Irish) strength.

Brie
(French) from Brie in France;
(Ir) strength. A short form of names
starting with 'Bri' e.g.
Brianna/Brianne/Brielle/Gabrielle.

Brielle
(French) she is from Brie in France;
(Ir) strength of God. A form of
Gabrielle.

Brienne
(Irish/Old English/Hebrew) strong
and graceful hill; (Ir) strong, graceful
and honourable. A feminine form
of Brian.

Brina
(Latin) boundary; (Ir) strength, virtue
and honour; (Eng) princess. A short
form of Sabrina.

Briona
(Irish/Old English) strong and
graceful hill; (Ir) strong and
honourable. A feminine
form of Brian.

Brita
(Irish) strong spirit; (Eng) from
Brittany in France

Britney/Brittany/Brittney
(Irish) from Brittany in France.

*Britt/Britta

(Irish) strong spirit; (Eng) from

Brittany; (Swed) strength. A short
form of Brittany/Brittney.

Bronwyn
(Welsh) white-haired friend.

*Brook/*Brooke
(Old English) stream.

*Brooklyn
(Old English) pool by the stream.

*Bryn
(Latin) boundary; (Wel) hill.

Bryna
(Latin) boundary; (Ir) strength,
virtue and honour; (Eng) princess.
A short form of Sabrina.

Bryony
(English) bear; (Ger) cottage; (Ir) hill;
strong and honourable. A feminine
form of Bryon/Brian.

Byanna
(Irish) hill; (Ir) strong and
honourable.

C

Cadence/*Cadie/*Cady
(Latin) rhythm; drum.

Caeley
(Arabic/Hebrew/Old English)
crown of laurel leaves in
the meadow; (O/Eng) pure meadow.

Caera
(Irish) brownish-red complexioned.

Cai
(Vietnamese) woman; (Ir) pure;
(Wel/Lat) happy.

Cailin
(Welsh/Irish) pure pool.

Caimile
(African) life continues.

Cainwen
(Welsh) fair-haired blessed one.

Caitlin/Caitlyn
(Irish/Latin) pure pool. The Irish
form of Catherine.

Cala
(Arabic) castle.

Calandra
(Greek) carefree; lark bird.

Calantha

(Greek) flower.

*Caley
(Irish/Old English/Scottish)
slender meadow.

Calida
(Spanish) warm and glowing.

Calla
(Greek) beautiful.

*Callan
(German) talker; (O/Nrs) to cry;
(Abor) sparrow hawk.

Callie
(Arabic) fortress.

Calliope
(Greek) muse; beautiful.

Callista
(Greek) beautiful.

Calypso
(Greek) concealing.

*Cam
(Vietnamese) sweet citrus;
(Gyp) loved; (Scot) crooked
or bent nose. A short form
of Cameron.

Cambria
(Latin) from Wales.

Camelia
(Latin) beautiful flower.

Camilla/Camille
(French) young ceremonial attendant;
messenger; (Arab) perfection.

Candace/Candice/Candra
(Greek) pure, white glow.

Cantrelle
(French) she is like a song.

Caprice
(Italian) fanciful.

Cara
(Italian) dearest.

*Carey
(Welsh) castle on the rocky island;
(O/Eng) caring; loving.

Cari
(Turkish) gentle, flowing stream.

Carina
(Spanish) little darling.

Carissa
(Greek) beloved.

Carita
(Latin) charity.

Carlissa
(German/Greek) strong and
courageous oath to God; honeybee.
A combination of Carla and Lisa.

Carly
(German) strong and courageous.
A short form of names starting
with 'Carl' e.g. Carlotta and a
feminine form of Carl/Charles.

Carmela
(Hebrew) vineyard; garden.

Carmen
(Latin) song.

Carra/Karra
(Irish) friend.

Carrie
(French/English) strong and
courageous. A short form of names
starting with 'Car' e.g. Caroline.

Carys/Caryss
(Welsh) love.

*Casey/*Kasey
(Irish) brave.

Cass/Cassie/Cassy
(Greek) prophet. A short form
of names starting with 'Cass'

e.g. Cassandra.

Cassandra/Kassandra
(Greek) prophet.

Cassia/Kassia
(Latin) flowering.

*Cassidy/*Kassidy
(Irish) clever; curly haired.

Cate
(Greek) pure. A short form

of Catherine.

Catelyn
(Irish/Latin) pure pool. A form of
Catherine.

Catherine/Catharine/Catherine
(Greek) pure.

Catriona/Catrina/Katrina
(Greek/Slavic) pure.

Cayla/Kayla
(English) pure; (Heb) laurel tree;
laurel leaves; victory.

Cayley
(Old English) pure meadow. A
combination of Cay/Kay and Lee.

Ceara
(Irish/Scottish) spearer.

Cecania
(German) free.

Ceinlys
(Welsh) gem.

Ceinwen
(Welsh) beautiful and precious
stone.

Celandine
(Latin/Greek) the little swallow bird;
a yellow flowering plant.

Celena/Celina/Selena/
Selina
(Latin/Greek) moon; heavenly.

Celeste
(Latin/French) heavenly.

Celestina/Celestine
(Latin/Old English) little one
from heaven.

Celie
(Latin/French) heavenly.

Celine
(Latin/French) moon; heavenly.

Celyren
(Welsh) holly.

Cera
(Irish/Welsh) reddish-brown
complexioned; belt.

Cerelia
(Latin) spring in the meadow.

Cerella/Cerelle
(Latin) springtime.

Ceres
(Roman) Goddess of the harvest;
(Lat) candle.

Ceridwen
(Welsh) poetry; white. The Welsh
Goddess of poetry.

Cerise
(French) cherry.

Cersei
(Greek) Goddess. A form of Circe.

Cerys
(Welsh) love. A form of Carys.

Chalee
(Hebrew/Old English) life meadow;
fairy meadow.

Chalice
(French) goblet.

Chambray
(French) light and delicate fabric.

Chanel/Chanelle
(French/English) she is from
the strait.

Chantal
(French) song.

Chantelle
(French) she is a song. A form
of Chantal.

Chantilly
(French) fine and delicate; lace.

Chapelle
(French) chapel. A form of Schapelle.

Charis
(French) tender; (Grk) graceful.

Charisse
(French) cherry.

*Charlie/Charlee/Charleigh/
*Charley/*Charly
(German/Old English) strong
and courageous one from
the meadow. A feminine form of
Charlie/Charles and a short
form of names starting
with 'Charl' e.g. Charlene.

Charlotte
(German/French) strong and
courageous. A feminine

form of Charles.

Charmain/Charmane
(Greek) little joyous one;
(Ger) singer.

Chavella/Chavelle
(Spanish) oath to God. A form
of Elizabeth.

Chavon
(Irish) God is gracious. A form
of Siobhain.

Chaya/Shaya
(Hebrew) life.

Chaylea/Shaylea
(Hebrew/Old English) life
meadow; fairy meadow.

Chen
(Chinese) precious.

Chenia
(Hebrew) God is gracious.

Chenoa
(Irish/Latin/French) she is unity,
she is one; (Nat/Amer) white dove.

Cherie
(French) beloved; cherry.

Cherilyn
(French/Welsh) cherry tree pool;
(O/Eng) beloved pool.

Cherise/Cherish
(French) beloved.

Chiara
(Italian) clear and bright.

Chilali
(Native American) snowbird.

Chimalis
(Native American) blue bird.

Chimene
(French) hospitable.

Chloe/Chloé
(Greek) flowering. A form of
Chloris.

Cholena
(Native American) bird.

Chontal
(French) song. A form of
Chantal.

Chrissanth
(French) golden flower.

Chrissy
(German/Greek/English) Christ
bearer; Christian; (Austral) Christmas.
A short form of names stating with
'Chris' e.g. Christine.

Christa
(German/Greek) Christ bearer;
Christian. A form of Christina.

Christabel/Christabella/
Christabelle
(Latin/French/Italian) beautiful
Christian; beautiful Christ bearer.
A combination of Christa and
Bell/Bella/Belle.

*Christen
(Greek) Christian; Christ bearer.
A form of Christina.

*Christian
(Greek) Christian; Christ bearer.
A form of Christina.

Christina/Christine
(Greek) little Christian; little Christ
bearer.

Chrysanthe
(Greek) golden flower. A form of
Chrysanthemum.

Chryseis
(Latin/Greek) golden; daughter
of the golden one.

Chu
(Chinese) pearl.

Chumani
(Sioux) dew drop.

Ciana
(Italian) God is gracious;
(Chin) China.

Ciara
(Irish) black; dark-haired.

Cicely
(Latin) unseeing. A form of
Cecelia.

*Cien
(Irish) ancient.

Cinnia
(Latin) curly-haired.

Clara
(Latin) bright.

Clare/Claire/Klaire/Klare
(Latin) bright.

Clarest
(French) brightest.

Claribell/Clarabell/Clarabella/
Clarabelle/Claribella/Claribelle
(Latin/French/Italian) bright and
beautiful. A combination of
Clara and Bella/Belle.

Clarice/Clarissa/
Clarisse
(French) bright. The French
form of Clara.

Clarita
(Spanish/Latin) bright. A form

of Clara.

Claudia
(French) little and weak. A feminine
form of Claude.

Clementine
(Greek) merciful.

Cleo
(Greek)

little and famous; proclaimer.
A short form of Cleopatra.

Cleone
(Greek) glorious.

Clover
(Old English) the clover plant;
luck.

Constance
(Latin) constant.

Cora
(Greek) girl.

Corabell/Corabella/Corabelle
(Greek/French/Italian) beautiful,
little girl. A combination of Cora
and Bella/Belle.

Coralee
(Greek/Old English) girl from
the meadow. A combination
of Cora and Lee.

Cordelia
(Irish) jewel from the sea.

Cordella
(Latin) warm hearted.

Coretta
(Greek) girl.

Cori
(Greek) girl.

Corina/Corrina
(Greek) girl.

Corinne
(French) hollow.

Cosima
(Greek) universal harmony. A
feminine form of Cosmo.

Courtney
(Old French) short nosed;

farmstead (O/Eng) court.

Cressida
(Greek) golden.

*Crisiant
(Welsh) crystal.

Crystal
(Latin) gem; ice; (Lat) clear.

Crystalin
(Latin/Welsh/English) crystal
pool; (Grk/Eng) ice pool;
gem pool.

Cynara
(Greek) artichoke; thistle.

Cynthia/Synthia
(Greek) moon.

Cyra
(Persian) sun.

Cyrena
(Greek) alluring; Siren.

D

Dae
(English) born during the daytime.

Daenerys
(English/Welsh) day lady.

Dahila
(Scandinavian) valley; (Eng) the
dahlia flower.

*Dai
(Japanese) great; (Eng) born during
the day.

Daisy
(English) the day's eye; the daisy
flower.

*Dale
(Old English) valley.

Damia
(Greek) Goddess of the forces of
nature.

Damica
(French) friendly.

Damita
(Spanish) noble.

*Dana
(English) bright day; from Denmark;
(Heb) God is my judge. A form of
Daniella.

Dani/Danni/*Danny
(Hebrew) God is my judge. A short form
names starting with 'Dani' e.g. Danielle
and a feminine form of Danny/Daniel.

Dania/Daniah
(Hebrew) God is my judge.

Danica/Danika
(Slavic) morning star.

Danice
(Hebrew) God is my gracious judge.
A combination of Danielle and
Janice.

Danielle/Daniella/Daniela
(Hebrew) God is my judge. A feminine form
of Daniel.

Danna
(English) bright day; from Denmark;
(Heb) God is my judge. A short form of
Daniella.

Daphne
(Greek) flower.

Dara
(Hebrew) compassionate.

Darah
(Greek/American) wealthy princess.
A combination of Daria and Sarah.

*Darby
(Irish) free; (Scand) deer estate.

Darcelle
(French) she is from the fortress;
she is dark.

*Darcy
(Irish) dark-haired; (Fren) fortress.

Darlene/Darleene
(French) little darling.

Dawn
(English) sunrise.

Daya
(Hebrew) bird; (Sans) compassionate.

Dayna
(English) bright day; from Denmark;
(Heb) God is my judge. A form of
Daniella.

Deana/Deanna
(Old English) valley; (Fren) leader.
A feminine form of Dean.

Deandra
(Latin) divine; (Eng) valley. A feminine
form of Dean.

*Del/*Dell/Delle
(English) valley.

Delana
(German) noble protector; (Old Fren)
night; (Lat) alder grove. A feminine
form of Delano.

*Delaney/*Delany
(French/Irish) elder tree grove;
(Eng) valley lane; (Ir) the challenger's
descendant.

Delia/Deliah
(Greek) visible.

Delilah
(Hebrew) one who broods.

Delphine
(Greek) dolphin; from Delphi.

Delsie

(English/Spanish) sorrowful. A
form of Delores.

Delta
(Greek) fourth born daughter; river
mouth.

*Dena
(Native American) valley.

*Deni
(French/Australian) follower of
Dionysus, the God of wine. A short
form of Denise and a feminine form

of Dennis.

Denna
(Anglo Saxon) valley.

*Derry
(Irish) red-haired; from Derry in
England.

Deveney/Devony
(Irish) poet. A feminine form of
Devon.

*Devon
(Old English) defender; from
Devonshire in England; (Ir) poet;
people of the deep valley.

Diana
(Latin) Goddess of the hunt, the
moon and fertility; (Eng) divine
and graceful.

*Dillian
(Latin) object of love and devotion.

Dinah
(Hebrew) free.

*Dion/Diona/Dione
(Greek) daughter of heaven and
earth; Goddess of love.

*Dior
(French) golden.

Divinia
(Latin) divine.

Dolores
(Spanish) sorrowful. A form
of Delores.

Dominica
(Latin) belonging to God. A feminine
form of Dominic.

*Drew
(Greek) strong and courageous. A
feminine form of Andrew.

E

*Eavan
(Irish) fair-haired; fete.

Edana
(Irish) desired; little fiery.

Edelina/Edeline
(German) noble.

*Eden
(Hebrew) delightful; paradise.

*Edian
(Hebrew) God's decoration.

*Eir
(Old Norse) peaceful healer.

Eira
(Welsh) snow.

Eiralys
(Welsh) snow drop.

Eirene
(Greek) peaceful.

Ela
(Polish/German) noble, kind and
cheerful. A form of Adelaide.

Elana
(Latin) spirited; (Heb) oak tree.

Elanora
(Aboriginal) seaside.

Eleanor
(Greek) light.

Elena
(Greek) light. The Italian form

of Helen.

Eleni
(Greek/Scottish) light. The Greek

form of Ellen.

Elenora/Elenore
(Greek/Scottish) light; (Haw)
bright.

Eleora
(Hebrew) God is my light.

Eletta
(English) elf.

Elga
(Gothic/Slavic) holy.

Eliana
(Hebrew) God has answered.

Elicia
(Hebrew) oath to God; truthful;
(Ger) noble. A form of Elisha.

Elidi
(Greek) sun gift.

Eliora
(Hebrew) light of God.

Elisa
(Spanish/Hebrew/English) oath
to God. A form of Elizabeth.

Elise/Eleece/Eleese/Elice
(French/English) oath to God. A
form of Elizabeth.

Elisha
(Hebrew) God is my salvation;
(Grk) truthful; (Ger) noble.

Elissa
(Greek/Hebrew) oath to God. A

short form of Elizabeth.

Elita
(Latin/French) special; chosen.

Eliza
(Hebrew) oath to God.
A short form of Elizabeth.

Elizabet/Elizabeta/Elizabeth
(Hebrew) oath to God.

*Elk
(Native American) deer;
(Haw) black.

Elka
(Polish/Hebrew) oath to God. A
short form of Elizabeth.

Elke
(German) noble.

Ella
(Old English) little fairy girl.

Ellaria
(Old English/Spanish) little fairy
of the river. A combination of
Ella and Ria.

Elle/Elli/Ellie/Elly
(French) she; (Scott/Grk) light.

Ellen

(Scottish/Greek) light. The
Scottish form of Helen.

Ellice
(Greek) noble.

Elodie
(Latin/German) wealthy;
flower.

Eloisa
(Italian/German) famous in
war.

Eloise
(German) healthy; (Fren) famous
in war.

Elsa
(German) noble; oath to God.
The Hebrew form of
Elizabeth.

Elsie
(German) noble; oath to
God. The Hebrew form
of Elizabeth.

Elva/Elvy
(English) elf.

Elvina/Elvine
(English) little elf.

Elvy/Elvie
(English) elf.

Emanuela/Emanuelle
(Hebrew) God is with us. A feminine
form of Emmanuel.

Emere
(Māori) hard working.

Emiliana
(French/Latin) binding; one who
flatters; (Ger) hard working. A
combination of Emma and Liana.

Emilia/Emilie/Emily/
Emilee/Emileigh
(French/Latin) flatterer; (Ger)
hard working. A short form
of Emmaline.

Emma/Emmalina/Emmaline
(French/Latin) flatterer; (Ger)
hard working.

Emmanuella/Emmanuelle
(Hebrew) God is with us. A feminine
form of Emmanuel.

Ena
(Irish) light. A form of Helen.

Enya
(Scottish) jewel; (Afr) fiery.

Epiphany/Epiphanes
(Hebrew) illustrious; born on
January 6th, a Christian festival.

Epona
(Gaul) horse Goddess.

Eponi
(Tongan) ebony; black.

Erela
(Hebrew) angel.

Erin/Erinna
(Irish) peace; from Ireland.

Estee
(Persian) star.

Estella/Estelle
(French/Latin) she is a star.

Etta/Ette/Ettie
(German) little. A short form of
names ending in 'etta' e.g. Annetta.

Eugania

(Greek/French/Hebrew) noble and
wellborn; God is gracious.

Eugenie
(Greek) noble and wellborn;
God is gracious. A feminine
form of Eugene.

Eva
(Hebrew) living. A form of Eve.

Evaline/Evalina
(Hebrew/French) living. A form
of Eve.

Evangelina/Evangeline
(Greek) angel, messenger of God.

Evania
(Irish) youthful warrior.

Evanthe
(Greek) flower.

Eve
(Hebrew) living.

Eveleen
(Irish) pleasant living.

Evelyn/Evelyna/Evelynna/
Evelynne
(Hebrew/Welsh) living pool.

Evetta/Evette
(French) young archer;
archer's bow; knight of the lion.
A form of Yvette
and a feminine form of Yves.

Evi/Evie
(Hungarian/Hebrew) life.
A form of Eve and a short
form of names starting with Eve,
for example, Evelynne.

Evita
(Spanish/Hebrew) life. A
form of Eve.

Evonne

(French) young archer. A
form of Yvonne.

F

*Fabayo
(Nigerian) lucky birth.

Fabrienne
(French) little blacksmith. A
feminine form of Fabron.

*Faina/Faine
(Old English/German) joy.

Fairlea/Fairlee/Fairleigh/
Fairley/Fairly
(Old English) light-coloured
meadow; fete meadow;
good meadow.

Faith
(Middle English) forever true.

Falda
(Icelandic) folding wings.

Faline
(Latin) cat-like. A form of Feline.

*Fallon
(Irish/Scottish) the ruler's
grandchild.

*Faren
(English) wandering.

Farrah
(Old English) pleasant; (Arab)
happiness.

Fayola
(Nigerian) lucky.

Fayre
(Old English) fair-haired; fete, good.

Fedora
(Greek) divine gift.

Felice
(Greek) happy; (Lat) fortunate. A

feminine form of Felix.

Felicia
(Latin) fortunate. A feminine form
of Felix.

Felicity/Felicitas
(English/Latin) fortunate.

Felora
(Hawaiian) flower. A form of
Flora.

Fenella/Fenelle
(Irish/Scottish) white-shouldered.

Fenna
(Norse/Irish) white-shouldered;
fair-haired.

Fern
(Old English) fern; feather. A short
form of names starting with
'Fern' e.g. Fernanda.

Fernlee/Fernleigh/Fernley
(Old English) fern meadow.

Feronia
(Etruscan) Goddess of flowers.

Filia
(Greek) friend; (Ital) one who
loves horses.

Filippina
(Italian) one who loves horses.

Filomena
(Greek/Italian) one who loves horses;
she is loved; love song. A form

of Philomena.

Finna
(Irish) fair-haired; (Nrs) white-
shouldered.

Finola
(Scottish) white-shouldered;
fair-haired.

Fionnula
(Scottish/Irish) fair-haired;
white-shouldered.

Fira
(English) fiery.

Fleur
(French) flower.

Fleurette
(French) little flower.

Flora
(Latin) flower. A short form of
Florence.

Florence
(Latin) blossoming flower.

Floria
(Latin/Basque) flower. A form
of Flora.

Florimel
(Greek) nectar; sweet.

Florine/Florina
(Latin) blossoming flower. A
form of Florence.

Fontane
(French) fountain.

Fontana/Fontanna
(French) fountain.

Fosetta
(French) dimpled.

Francesca
(Latin/Italian) free; from France;
(Eng) honest. A form of Frances.

Francine
(English) honest; (Lat) freedom;
from France. A feminine form
of Frank.

Freya
(Scandinavian) noble lady. The
Norse Goddess of love.

G

Gaea/Gaia
(Greek) earth.

Galanthe
(Greek) cream-coloured.

Galena
(Greek) calm healer.

Gali/*Galie/Galli/
*Gallie
(Hebrew) spring or fountain
on a hill.

Galina
(Russian) light; (Grk) calm. The
Russian form of Helen.

*Garyn
(English) spearer. A form of Gary/
Garry.

Gem/Gemma
(Latin) gem.

Genevieve
(Welsh/French) white wave; woman
of the people.

Georgia/Georgie
(Latin/Greek) farmer. A short form
of Georgina.

*Germain/Germaine
(French) from Germany.

Gervaise
(French) spear skilled.

Gia
(Italian) God is gracious. A short form of
Giacinta.

Giacinta
(Italian) hyacinth; purple; precious
white gem. A form of Jacinta.

Giacobba
(Hebrew) maintainer. A feminine
form of Jacob.

*Gian/*Gyan
(Italian/Hebrew) God is gracious.
A form of Jane.

Gianna
(Italian/Hebrew) God is gracious.
A form of Jane.

Gigi
(German) brilliant.

Gilda
(Old English) covered in gold;
(Ir) God's servant.

Gillian
(Latin) young bird; (Lat) youthful.
A feminine form of Julian.

*Gilly
(Gypsy) song.

Giordana/Giordane

(Italian/Hebrew) descending.

Giovanna
(Italian) God is gracious. A form
of Jane.

Giralda
(German) spear ruler.

Gisela/Giselle
(English) protector with a sword;
(Ger) promise.

Gitana
(Spanish) Gypsy.

Gloria/Glorien/Glory
(Latin) magnificent.

Grace/Gracia/Gratiana
(Latin) graceful.

Greer
(Greek/Scottish) watchful.
The Scottish feminine form
of Gregory.

Greta
(Greek) pearl; (Eng) daisy. The
Slavic, Swedish and German forms
of Margaret.

Gretchen
(Greek/German) pearl. A form
of Margaret.

Gretel
(Greek) pearl.

Guinevere
(Welsh) white wave.

Gypsy
(Old English) wanderer.

H

Hadlea/Hadlee/Hadleigh/
*Hadley/*Hadly
(English) heather meadow.

Haidee
(Greek) modest.

Hailea/Hailee/Haileigh/
*Hailey/*Haley
(Scottish) hero; (O/Eng)
hay meadow.

Halina
(Hawaiian) resemblance.

Halle
(Scandinavian/English) hero;
(O/Eng) hall meadow.

Hallie
(Greek) one who thinks of the sea;
(O/Eng) hall meadow. A short
form of Halimeda.

Halona
(Native American) fortunate;
(Haw) army power.

Hana
(Hawaiian) work; (Jap) blossom flower;
(Heb) God is gracious; merciful. A
form of Hannah.

Hannah
(Hebrew) God is gracious; merciful.

*Hanniel
(Hebrew) gift of God. A form of
Danielle and a feminine form
of Daniel.

*Hanya
(Aboriginal) stone.

Haylea/Haylee/Hayleigh/
*Hayley
(Old English) hay meadow.

Heather
(Middle English) heather; grass.

Heidi
(Swiss) noble; kind; cheerful. A short
form of Adelaide.

Helena
(Greek) light.

Heloise
(German/French) famous warrior;
healthy; flourishing. The French
form of Eloise/Louise.

Hermione
(Greek) daughter of the earth.

Hialeah
(Cherokee) beautiful meadow;
(Eng) high meadow.

*Hollace/*Hollice/*Hollis
(Old English) holly tree grove.

Hollee/Holley/Holli/

Hollie/Holly
(Old English) holly.

Hope
(Old English) hope; desire.

Hyacinth
(Greek) hyacinth; purple.

I

*Ia
(Irish) yew tree.

Iantha/Ianthe
(Greek) violet coloured flower.

Ida
(Old English) prosperous,
hardworking and happy.

Idell/Idella/Idelle
(Irish) bountiful.

Ila
(Greek/Hungarian) light;
(O/Fren) island.

Ilana
(Hebrew) tree.

Ilene
(Irish) light.

Iliana
(Greek) from Troy; light;
(Heb) God has answered.

Ilona
(Hungarian) light; beautiful.

Ilsa
(German) noble.

Ilysa
(Latin) blissful.

Ilyssa
(Greek) logical.

Imala
(Native American) strong mind.

*Iman
(Arabic) believer.

Imogene
(Latin) image, likeness; (Ir) she is

the image of her mother.

Ina
(Irish) pure. A form of Agnes.

*Inari
(Finnish) lake.

Inas
(Polynesian) wife of the moon.

*India
(Hindi) from India.

*Indigo
(Latin) dark blue/violet colour.

Indira
(Hindi) great.

Inga
(Scandinavian) beautiful daughter
of the hero.

Inge
(Old Norse) meadow; (O/Eng)
to extend.

Ingrid
(Scandinavian) beautiful daughter
of the hero.

*Inola
(Cherokee) black fox.

Ioana
(Romanian/Hebrew) God is
gracious.

Iola
(Greek) violet-coloured flower;

(Wel) worthy of the lord.

Iolana
(Hawaiian) soaring hawk.

Iolanda
(Greek/French) violet flower;
purple. A form of Yolanda.

*Ione
(Greek) violet-coloured stone.

*Ireland
(Irish/Old English) from
Ireland; peace; Erin.

Irena/Irene/Iriny
(Greek) peaceful.

Iris
(Greek) rainbow; the iris
flower.

Isabella/Isabelle
(Spanish) dedicated to
God.

Isadora
(Greek) gift of Isis; (Eng)
adored. A feminine form of
Isidore.

Isola
(Italian) island.

Isolde

(Welsh) fair; (O/Ger)
ruler.

Ivy
(Old English) ivy vine.

J

Jacinda/Jacinta
(Greek) beautiful; (Heb)
maintainer; (Span/Grk) hyacinth;
purple. A form of Jacinta and
a feminine form of Jacinto.

*Jacoby
(Latin) maintainer. A form
of Jacob.

Jacqueline/Jaclyn
(Hebrew/French) maintainer. A
feminine form of Jacques/Jack.

Jada
(Hebrew) wise.

*Jade
(Spanish) precious green gemstone.

*Jae/*Jay/Jaye
(Latin) jay bird.

Jaia
(Hindi) victorious; God has
enlightened; illuminated river.
A feminine form of Jai.

Jaime/Jaimè/Jaimee/
*Jamie/*Jamey
(French) I love; (Heb) maintainer.

Jalena
(Latin) temptress; (Heb) God is
gracious. A form of Jane.

Jamilee
(Hebrew/Old English) meadow
maintainer. A combination of
Jami and Lee and a feminine

form of James.

Jana
(Hebrew/Slavic) God is gracious.
A form of Jane.

Jane
(Hebrew) God is gracious.
A feminine form of John.

Jasmine
(Persian) the jasmine flower.

Jayne/Jaine/Jayn
(Sanskrit) victorious; (Heb) God
is gracious. A form of Jane.

Jelena
(Russian) light. A form of Helen.

Jemima
(Hebrew) dove of peace.

Jemina
(Hebrew/Czech) jewel of the
earth.

Jemma/Jem/Jema
(English) jewel.

Jena
(Arabic) small bird; (Wel) fair-
haired; white wave. A form
of Jennifer.

Jenelia
(Welsh/Old English) fair-haired;

white wave in the meadow.
A combination of Jennifer
and Lea.

Jenica
(Hebrew) God is gracious.

Jenilea/Jenilee/Jenileigh/
Jeniley/Jennilea/Jennilee/
Jennileigh/ Jennili/Jennilie/Jennily
(Welsh) white wave in the meadow.

Jenna
(Welsh) fair-haired; white wave.

Jennalyn
(Welsh) white wave in the pool;
fair-haired one from the pool.
A combination of Jenna and Lyn.

Jennica/Jennika
(Welsh/English) white wave;

fair-haired.

Jennifer/Jennyfer
(Cornish) white wave; fair-haired.

*Jermaine
(French/German) from
Germany.

Jessenia
(Arabic) flower.

Jessica
(Hebrew) wealthy.

Jessi/*Jessie/*Jesse/
*Jessy
(Hebrew) wealthy. A short
form of names starting with
'Jess' e.g. Jessica.

*Jett/*Jette
(Danish) black; dark haired.

Jiana

(Hebrew/American/English)
graceful.

Jillaine
(Latin) youthful.

Jilli
(Aboriginal) today.

Jillian/Gillian
(Latin) youthful.

Jinny
(Welsh) white wave; fair-haired. A

form of Jenny/Jennifer.

*Jo
(Hebrew) God is gracious. A short
form of names starting with
'Jo' e.g. Joanna or Joby.

Joanna/Joanne
Hebrew) God is gracious. A
combination of Jo and Anne.

Jobeth
(Hebrew) from the gracious house
of God; oath to God. A combination
of Jo and Beth.

Jobina
(Hebrew) sorrowful. A feminine
form of Job.

*Joby
(Hebrew) sorrowful. A form
of Job.

*Jocasta
(Greek) shining moon; (Ital) lighthearted.

Joia/Joya
(French) happiness.

Jolena
(French) pretty.

*Jordaine
(Hebrew) river of judgement;

descending. A feminine form
of Jordan.

*Jordan
(Hebrew) river of judgement;
descending.

*Jori
(Hebrew) casting forth; child
bornat the time of the autumn/fall rains.
A form of Jora.

Josephina/Josephine
(Hebrew) God has added a

child; increasing; perfect. A
feminine form of Joseph.

Josette
(Hebrew/French) God has
added a little child; increasing;
perfect. A feminine form of Jose.

Josee/Josi/Josie
(Hebrew/French) God has added
a child; increasing; perfect. A
feminine form of Jose.

Jovanna
(Latin) love; majestic and graceful;
(Heb/Lat) joyful and graceful. A

feminine form of Jovan and a
combination of Jovi and Anna.

Joy/Joi/Joia/Joya
(Latin) happiness.

Juana/Juanita
(Spanish) God is gracious. A
feminine form of Juan/John.

Julia/Julie
Latin) youthful. A feminine
form of Julius.

Julianna/Julianne
(Latin/Slavic/Hungarian/
Spanish/Hebrew) youthful
and graceful.

Juliet/Julieta/Juliett/
Julietta/Juliette
(Latin/French) little and
youthful.

K

*Kachine
(Native American) ceremonial
dance.

*Kacie/*Kacy
(Irish) alert.

*Kai
(Navajo) willow tree; (Haw) sea;
(Jap) to forgive; (Wel) keeper
of the keys.

Kaila/Kailah
(Tongan) to call out; (Isra) victory;
crown of laurel leaves.

Kailani
(Hawaiian) sky; sea.

Kaimana
(Hawaiian) diamond.

Kaitlin/Kaitlyn
(English/Welsh) pure pool.

*Kal

(Navajo) willow; (Eng) yellow
flower.

Kala
(Hawaiian) sun; (Hin) black;
time.

Kalala
(Hawaiian) bright.

Kalama
(Hawaiian) torch; flames.

Kalani
(Hawaiian) sky.

Kalea/Kalee/Kaleigh/Kaley
(Hawaiian) bright.

Kalei
(Hawaiian) pure wreath

of flowers; (O/Eng) pure meadow.

Kali
(Sanskrit) energy; (Haw) one
who hesitates.

Kalia
(Tongan) double canoe.

Kalila
(Arabic) loved; darling.

Kalina
(Wemba-Wemba) one who loves;
(Pol) flower.

Kalinda
(Aboriginal) view; (Sans) sun.

Kalinn
(Scandinavian) river.

Kalla
(Aboriginal) fiery.

*Kallan
(Scandinavian) flowing water.

Kalliope/Calliope
(Greek) beautiful; muse.

Kallista
(Greek) beautiful.

Kamille/Camille
(French) young ceremonial
attendant; messenger; (Arab)
perfection.

*Kani
(Hawaiian) sound.

Kara
(Aboriginal) possum; (Turk)
black.

Karis/Karissa/Carys/
Caryss
(Greek) graceful; favourite;
(Wel) love.

Karla/Carla
(German) strong and courageous.

A form of Carla and a feminine form
of Charles.

Karli
(Turkish) covered in snow.

Karri
(Aboriginal) eucalyptus tree.

Karrin
(Aboriginal) evening time; (Grk)
pure. A form of Karen.

Kasimira
(Slavic) peace maker; honour;
glory. A feminine form of Casimir.

Kassandra/Cassandra
(Greek) prophet.

Kassia
(Greek) pure; (Heb) cassia tree.

*Kassidy/*Cassidy

(Irish) clever; curly haired.

Kate/Katie
(Greek) pure. A short form of
Katherine/Catherine.

Kateri
(Native American) saint; (Grk)
pure harvester. A combination of
Kate and Teri.

Katherine/Katheryn
(Greek) pure.

Katina
(Aboriginal) first born; (Grk/O/Eng)
little and pure.

Katrina
(Scandinavian/Swedish/Slavic/
Lithuanian/Australian) pure.
A form of Katherine.

Katrinelle
(Greek/French) she is pure.

Kaya
(Hopi) elder sister; wisdom;
(Jap) place of rest.

Kayla
(English) pure; (Heb) laurel tree;
laurel leaves; victory.

Kaylea/Kayleah/Kaylee/
Kayleigh
(Greek/Old English) pure
meadow.

*Keely
(Irish) beautiful.

*Keena
(Irish) brave and quick; (Eng)
eager.

*Kei
(Hawaiian) glorious.

Keighlea

(Irish/Old English) pure meadow.

Keija
(Greek/Swedish) pure. A form
of Katherine.

Keilani
(Hawaiian) glorious chief.

Keina
(Aboriginal) moon.

*Kelby
(Scandinavian) fountain spring.

*Kele
(Hopi) sparrow hawk;
(Tong) clay.

Kelesi
(Tongan) grace.

*Kelsey
(Old Norse) ship island.

*Kennedy
(Old English) royal ruler; (Ir)
helmeted chief.

Kennice
(Old English) beautiful. A
feminine form of Kenneth.

Keona
(Irish) beautiful.

Khaleesi
(Tongan) grace; wife of the Khal.
A form of Kelesi. Nigerian praise
to God. A form of Kalechi.

Kimana
(Shoshone) butterfly.

Kimiko
(Japanese) heavenly and
righteous child.

*Kina
(Hawaiian) little one; china.

The Hawaiian form of Tina.

*Kinta
(Choctaw) beaver; (Abor)
laughing.

Kioko
(Japanese) born in
happiness.

Kira/Kirra
(Māori) tree bark; (Abor) fireplace;
magpie; (Russ) lady; (Bulg) throne.

*Kirby
(Old English) church by the farm;
cottage near the water.

*Kiri
(Māori) tree bark.

Kirra
(Aboriginal) magpie; fireplace.
Kirsten
(Scottish) anointed in oil.

Koo
(Greek) pure. A short form of
Katherine.

Kristen/Kristian
(Scandinavian) Christian; Christ
bearer. The Scandinavian form of
Kristine/Christine.

Kristianna
(Scandinavian) graceful Christian;
graceful Christ bearer. A
combination of Kristian and Anna.

Kyrene
(Greek) lord.

Kyrie
(Irish) dark-haired.

L

Lacey
(English) delicately woven web
like fabric; (Lat) cheerful.

Laella/Laelle
(French/English) the elf.

Laflora
(French/Latin) the flower.

Laili
(Arabic) dark beauty of the night;
dark-haired; born during the
night. A form of Layla.

Laine/Layn/Layne
(English) light; little road.

Lainey/Lanie
(French) wool; (Eng) light; little
road. A short form of Elaine.

Laka
(Hawaiian) alluring.

Lake
(Latin) large pond.

Lakia
(Arabic) treasure.

Lala
(Slavic) tulip flower.

Lali
(Polynesian) the highest point of
heaven; (Tong) wooden drum.

Lalita
(Sanskrit) pleasing and charming,

playful; (Grk) talkative.

Lallee/Lalleigh/Lalli/
Lallie/Lally
(English) talker.

Lami
(Tongan) hidden.

Lana
(Latin) woolly; (Haw) light and
airy; (Ir/Scott) harmony; peace; fair
and beautiful. A short form of Alana/Alannah.

*Lane/*Lain/Laine/
*Layn/Layne
(Middle English) narrow road;
(Abor) good.

Lanelle
(Old French) she is from the little
road.

Lanet
(Scottish) little and graceful.

Lani
(Hawaiian) sky; heaven.

Lara
(Latin) shining and famous; (Abor)

48

hut built on stones; (Grk) happy.

Larana
(Latin) sea bird.

Lareina
(Spanish) queen.

Lari
(Latin) holy; (Lat) victory; crown
of laurel leaves. A short form of
names starting with 'Lari' e.g.
Larissa/Lariana.

Lariana
(Latin/Hebrew) graceful and
holy; graceful victory. A
combination of Lari
and Anna.

Laricia
(Latin) holy; victory, crown of
laurel leaves.

Lariel
(Hebrew) God's lion; light of
God. A form of Ariel.

Larina
(Latin) sea bird.

Larine/Laryne
(Latin) girl from the sea;
(Lat) sorrowful; (Fren)
from Lorraine in France;
(Ger) famous warrior; (O/Eng)
crown of laurel leaves in the rain;
victory in the rain. A form
of Lorraine.

Larissa
(Latin) laurel tree; laurel leaves;
victory; (Grk) happy. A form of
Lorissa.

Lark
(Middle English) carefree; lark
bird; (Abor) cloud.

Larni

(Hawaiian) heavenly child; sky.

Laroux
(French) red-haired.

Latania
(French/Russian) queen of
the fairies. A form of Tatania/
Titania.

Latara
(Irish/American) rocky hill. A
form of Tara.

Laulani
(Hawaiian) heavenly branch.

Laura
(Latin) laurel tree; leaves; victory.

Lauralea/Loralee/Loraleigh/
Lorali/Loralie
(Latin/Old English) laurel tree
meadow; meadow of victory. A
combination of Laura and Lee.

Laurel
(Latin) laurel tree; laurel leaves;
victory.

Lauren
(Latin) laurel tree; laurel leaves;
victory.

Lavinia
(Latin) pure.

Lavonna
(French/American) the archer. A
form of Yvonne.
Layla/Laylah/Laila/

Lailah
(Persian/Arabic) dark beauty of the
night; dark-haired; born during the
night.

Layna
(Greek) light.

Lea/Leah/Lee/
Leigh/Ley
(Old English) meadow; (Heb) tired;
(Lat) lion-like.

Leandra
(Latin/Greek) lion-like; faithful.

Leanore
(Greek/Scottish) light; (Haw) bright.

*Lei
(Hawaiian) heavenly child; garland
of flowers; (Tong) ivory;
whale's tooth.

*Leigh/*Lee/*Ley
(Old English) meadow.

Leila
(Persian/Arabic) dark beauty of the
night; dark-haired; born during the night.
A form of Layla.

Leilani
(Hawaiian) child of heavenly flowers.

Lelei
(Tongan) wonderful.

Lelia
(Greek) fair speech.

Lelya
(Russian) light. The Greek form
of Helen.

Lenci
(Hungarian) light.

Lene
(German) light. The Greek form
of Helen.

Leni
(Latin) alluring one, Siren; light.
A short form of Helena.

Lenia
(German) lion-like. A feminine
form of Leon.

Lenice
(German) bold strength; lion-
like. A feminine form
of Leonard.

Lenore
(Greek) light. A form of
Eleanor/Helen.

Leona
(French) lion-like.

Leotie
(Native American) flower on
the prairie.

Leura
(Aboriginal) lava; (Eng) valley.

Levania
(Latin) morning sun.

Levona
(Hebrew) spice; incense.

Lexa
(Czech/Greek) defender of
humankind. A short form of
Alexandra and a feminine form
of Lex/Alex/Alexander.

Lexi/Lexia
(Greek) defender of humankind.
A short form of Alexandra and
a feminine form of Lex/
Alex/Alexander.

*Leya
(Spanish) loyalty; law.
Leyla/Leylah/Layla/Laylah
(Persian/Arabic) dark beauty of the
night; dark-haired; born during the
night. A form of Layla.

Lia
(Hebrew/Dutch/Italian) dependent;
(Grk) she brings good news.

Liah
(Old English/Hebrew) meadow.
A form of Lea/Leah/Lee.

Liama
(German) helmet of resolution;
(Ir) willful. The Irish feminine
form of Liam/William.

Lian
(Chinese) graceful willow.

Liana
(French) binding.

Lien
(Chinese) lotus flower.

Liese
(German) oath to God. A form of
Elizabeth.

Liesel
(German/Hebrew) oath to God. A
form of Elizabeth.

Lily/Lilly/Lillie
(Latin) the lily flower.

Lilybell/Lilybella/Lilybelle/
Lillybell/Lillybella/Lillybelle
(Latin/Old English) beautiful lily.
A combination of Lily and Belle.

Lilybet
(Latin/Old English) oath to God.
A form of Elizabeth.

*Lin
(Burmese) bright; (Chin) beautiful
jade stone; (Wel) pool. A short
form of names starting with
'Lin' e.g. Lindel.

Lina
(Italian/Spanish) light.

*Linden
(Old English) lime tree valley.

Linlea/Linlee/Linleigh
(Old English) pool meadow; flax
meadow; linden tree meadow. A
combination of Lin and Leigh.

Linnea
(Scandinavian) linden/lime tree;
(Swed) flower.

Liolya
(Russian) light. A form of Helen.

Liona
(Latin/English) lion-like.

Liora/*Lior
(Hebrew) light.

*Lira
(Aboriginal) river.

*Liron
(Hebrew) the song is mine.

Lirra
(Aboriginal) wren.

Lis
(French) lily.

Lise
(Greek) honeybee; (Heb/Ger)
oath to God. A short form of
Melissa/Elizabeth.

Lisle
(Old English) island. A feminine
form of Lyle.

Liss
(Scottish) from the court.

Liv
(Latin) olive branch; peace; (Eng)
holy. A short form of Olivia.

Livana
(Hebrew) white like the moon; (Lat)
graceful olive branch; peace. A
combination of Liv and Anna.

Livia
(Hebrew) joining; (Lat) olive branch;
peace; (Eng) holy. A form of Olivia.

Livona
(Hebrew) spice.

Lizabeth
(Hebrew/English) oath to God. A form
of Elizabeth.

Llian
(Welsh) linen.

*Logan
(Irish/Scottish) hollow.

Loila
(Aboriginal) sky.

Lois
(Greek/German) famous warrior.
A form of Louise and a feminine
form of Louis.

*Loke
(Hawaiian) rose.

Lola
(Spanish) strength.

Lolita
(Spanish) sorrow.

Lomasi
(Native American) pretty flower.

Lona/Lonee
(Middle English) solitary.

Loni
(English) solitary; (Lat) lion-like.

Lora
(Latin) alluring; wine; (Lat) laurel

leaves; laurel tree; victory. A form
of Laura.

Lore/Loree
(Latin) alluring; (Eng) folklore;
(Lat) laurel tree; laurel leaves; victory.
A short form of Lorelei.

Lorelei
(Latin/German) alluring; (Lat) laurel

trees; laurel leaves; victory.

Loren/Lorena
(Latin) laurel trees; laurel leaves;
victory. A form of Lauren.

Lorett
(Latin/English) little laurel trees;
little laurel leaves; little victory.

Loretta/Lorette
(Latin/English) little laurel trees;
little laurel leaves; little victory.

Lori/Loree
(Latin/English/American) alluring;
(Lat) laurel tree; laurel leaves; victory.
A short form of Lorelei and Lorraine.

Lorianna
(Latin/English/American/Hebrew)
graceful and alluring Siren; graceful
laurel tree; graceful laurel leaves. A
combination of Lori and Anna.

*Loric
(Latin) armour.

*Lorice
(Latin) laurel tree; laurel leaves;
victory.

Loricia
(Latin/Greek) holy laurel tree; holy
laurel leaves; holy victory.

Lorielle
(Latin/French) she has a crown

of laurel leaves; she has a crown
of victory; she is alluring.

Lorilei
(Latin/German) alluring; (Lat)
laurel trees; laurel leaves; victory.

Lorina
(Latin/German) alluring; (Lat) laurel
trees; laurel leaves; victory.

*Loris
(Greek) flowering; pale; (Dut) clown.
A form of Chloris/Chloe.

Lorissa
(Latin) laurel tree; laurel leaves;
victory; (Grk) happy.

Lorrelle
(Latin/German/French) little
laurel tree; little laurel leaves;

little victory; (Fren/O/Eng) she
is victorious.

Losa
(Polynesian) rose.

Louisa/Louise
(German/French) famous warrior.
A feminine form of Louis.

*Lorde/*Lourde/*Lourdes
(French) from Lourdes in France;
holy. A place where the Virgin Mary is
believed to have appeared.

Lovinia
(Latin) pure. A form of Lavinia.

*Luca
(Latin/Italian) bringer of light;
(Heb) rising to her; of light. A
feminine form of Lucas/Luke.

Lucia
(Latin) bringer of light; (Heb) rising
to her; of light. A feminine form of
Lucius.

Lucinda/Lucinta
(Latin) bringer of light; purple light;
(Heb) rising to her; of light.

Lucindee
(Latin) bringer of light from the
ashes; purple light; (Heb) rising to

her; of light. A feminine form
of Lucius and a combination
of Lucy and Cindee/Cindy.

Lucine
(Arabic) moon.

Lucretia
(Latin) rewarded.

Luella/Luelle/Luetta/
Luette
(Old English/French) little
and famous.

Luisa
(Spanish/German/French) famous
warrior. A feminine form of Louis.

*Lukia
(Latin/African) light; beginning of
the season; (Māori) slow. A
combination of Lucy/Luke
and Kia.

Lulani
(Hawaiian/Māori) highest point
of heaven.

*Lulie
(Middle English) sleepy.

Lulu/Loulou/Lou Lou
(Native American) rabbit; (Tong)
owl; (Arab) pearl; (Eng)
soothing; fairy.

*Lupe
(Spanish/Mexican) wolf;
(Haw) ruby.

Lyla
(Old English/French) island. A
feminine form of Lyle.

Lyris
(Greek) player of the harp; lyrical.

Lysandra
(Greek) defender of humankind. A
form of Alexandra/Sandra

and the feminine form
of Alexander.

Lyzabeth
(Hebrew) oath to God. A form
of Elizabeth.

M

Mabel
(Latin) worthy of love; lovable
beauty; (Ir) joy; queen of the fairies.
A short form of Amabel.

Macia
(Polish/Hebrew) bitter.

*Mackenna/*Makenna
(Scottish) child of the wise and
beautiful leader. A feminine form
of Mackenzie.

*Mackenzie/*Makenzie
(Scottish) child of the wise and
beautiful leader.

*Maddox
(Welsh) fortunate.

Madeleine/Madelaine
(Greek) high tower; (Eng) from
Magdalen or Magdala in England.

Madelena
(Greek) high tower.

*Madison
(Old English) child of the
powerful warrior.

Maemi
(Japanese) smile of truth.

Maeve
(Irish) joy; (Fren) songbird; (Gae)
delicate; (Eng) pale purple. A
form of Mauve.

Magdalen
(Greek/Hebrew) high tower.

Magena
(Native American) the coming
moon.

Maggie
(Greek) pearl. A form of
Margaret.

Magnolia
(Latin) the magnolia tree or
flower.

Mahal
(Malaysian) love.

Mahala
(Native American) woman of
power; (Heb) barren.

Mahalia
(Hebrew) affectionate; tender.

Mahina
(Hawaiian/Tongan) moonlight.

Mahira
(Hebrew) energy and speed.

Mai
(Navajo) coyote; (Jap) bright;
(Viet) flower.

Maia
(Greek) Goddess of spring;
bright star; mother; (Eng) woman.

Maire
(Irish/Hebrew) sea of bitterness; lady
of the sea. A form of Mary.

Mairead
(Irish/French) judge.

Mairi
(Hebrew) sea of bitterness; lady of the
sea. A form of Mary.

Maisie
(French) maize, sweet corn; pearl.
The Scottish form of Margaret.

Makayla
(Greek/Old English) pure; (Heb)
laurel tree; laurel leaves; victory. A
form of Kayla/Cayla.

Makedde/Makaidde
(Scottish/Greek) pure daughter.
A combination of Mack and Katie.

*Malachie
(French) messenger; angel. A
feminine form of Malach.

Malana
(Hawaiian) light; (Ir/Scott) harmony;
peace; fair and beautiful; bright and
cheerful. A form of Alanna and a
feminine form of Alan.

Malania
(Greek) dark-haired.

Malaya
(Malaysian) free; from Malaysia.

Mali
(Thai) jasmine flower.

Malia
(Zuni/Hawaiian) sea of bitterness;
lady of the sea. A form of Mary.

Maliaka
(Hawaiian) sea of bitterness; lady
of the sea. A form of Mary.

Malie
(Tongan) sweet.

Malika
(Hungarian) hard working.

Malina
(Hebrew) highly praised; (Haw) peace.

Malini
(Hindi) gardener. The Hindi God of
earth.

*Mallory
(French) armoured; wild duck;
(Lat) hammer; (O/Ger) army advisor.

Manetta/Manette
(French/Hebrew) little and wished; star
of the sea; bitter. A form of Mary.

Mani
(Chinese) prayer.

Manuela
(Spanish) God is with us. A
feminine form of Emmanuel.

Manya
(Russian/Hebrew) sea of bitterness;
lady of the sea. A form of Mary.

Mara

(Aboriginal) black duck.

Marabel
(English/Hebrew/French) beautiful
sea of bitterness; beautiful lady of the
sea; (Lat) worthy of love; lovable
beauty; (Ir) joy; queen of the fairies.
A combination of Mary/Mabel.

Marah
(Hebrew) melody.

Marcella
(Latin) war-like; warrior. A feminine
form of Marcel/Marc/Mark.

Marcie/Marcey/Marcy
(Latin) war-like; warrior. A form of
Marcella and a feminine form of
Marcel/Marc/Mark.

*Mardell
(Old English) meadow near the
marshland.

*Marden
(Old English) valley marshland.

*Mardi
(French) born of a Tuesday.

*Maren
(Latin) sea.

Margaery
(Greek) pearl. A form of Margery
or Margaret.

Margaux
(Greek/French) pearl. A form of
Margaret.

Marguerite/Marguarite
(Greek/French) pearl. A form of
Margaret.

Mari
(Japanese) ball; (Heb) sea of

bitterness; lady of the sea. The
Spanish form of Mary.

Maria/Mariah
(Hebrew/French) sea of bitterness;
lady of the sea. A form of Mary.

Mariabella
(Hebrew/Italian) beautiful sea of
bitterness; beautiful lady of the sea.
A combination of Maria and Bella.

Maribel
(Hebrew) beautiful sea of bitterness;
beautiful lady of the sea. A
combination of Mary and Belle.

*Marice
(German/French) marsh flower;
dark-haired one from the marshland.
A form of Maurice.

Marie/Maree
(Hebrew/French) sea of bitterness; lady
of the sea. A form of Mary.

Mariel
(Hebrew/German/Dutch) sea
of bitterness; lady of the sea. A
form of Mary.

Marigold
(Hebrew/English) Mary's gold; a
flower with yellow/orange petals;
sea of bitterness; lady of the sea.

Marika
(Hebrew/Dutch/Slavic) sea of
bitterness; lady of the sea. A form of
Mary.

Marilee
(Hebrew/Old English) bitter meadow;
star of the sea meadow. A
combination of Mary and Lee.

Marilla
(Hebrew/German) sea of bitterness;
lady of the sea. A form of Mary.

Marina
(Latin) of the sea; where boats moor.

Marinna
(Aboriginal) song.

Maris
(Latin) from the sea; dark-haired
one from the marshland. A feminine
form of Maurice.

Mariska
(Hebrew) sea of bitterness; lady
of the sea. A form of Mary.

Marisol
(Spanish) sunny sea.

Marita
(Latin/Spanish) sea.

Marjolaine
(French) marjoram.

Marlea/Marlee/Marleigh/
Marley
(Aboriginal) elder tree; (O/Eng)
meadow marshland.

Marlene
(Hebrew) praised highly; (Grk)
high tower. A form of Madeline.

*Marling
(Hebrew/Welsh) wished for pool;
bitter pool; star of the sea pool.
A combination of Mary and
Lin/Lyn.

*Marlis
(Hebrew/English) oath to God.

*Marlow
(Old English) hill by the lake.

Marney/Marni/Marnie/

Marny
(Israeli) rejoicing.

*Marquise
(French) noble.

Marquita
(French) canopy.

Marree
(Aboriginal) place of possums.

Marya
(Arabic) bright white; pure; (Heb)
sea of bitterness; lady of the sea.
A form of Mary.

Maryelle
(Hebrew/Greek) wished for light;
star light of the sea; bitter light. A
combination of Mary and Ellen.

Matilda
(German) strong and powerful warrior.

Mauve
(Greek) soft, violet-coloured.

*Maverick
(English/American) independent;
spirited.

Mavia
(Irish) joy. Mavis (French)
songbird.

May
(Latin) great one, pink and
white blossom; born in
the month of May.

Maya
(Hindi) creative power of God;
(Grk) mother or grandmother;
(Lat) great.

Maybelle
(Latin) great; worthy of love;
beautiful one born in May. A
combination of May and Bell.

Mayda
(English) woman; born in May.

Mayoree
(Thai) beautiful; (Heb) sea of

bitterness; lady of the sea. A
form of Mary.

Mayra
(Aboriginal) wind of spring.

Maysun
(Arabic) beautiful; (O/Fren) stone
mason. A feminine form of Mason.

*Mckenzie/*Mackenzie
(Scottish) child of the wise and
beautiful leader.

Mead/Meade
(Greek) honey wine; (O/Eng)
meadow.

Meagan
(Irish/Greek/Welsh) great; (Ir)
strength; pearl; (Fren) daisy. The

Irish and Scottish form of
Margaret.

Meara
(Scottish) laughter; (Eng) pool.

Meave
(Irish) joy; (Grk) soft, violet-
coloured. A form of Maeve.

Mee
(Chinese) beautiful.

Meena
(Greek) her mother's gift.

Meg
(Greek) little pearl. A short form
of Margaret.

Megan
(Irish/Greek) great; (Ir) strength;

(Fren) daisy. A form of Margaret.

Mei
(Hawaiian) great; (Chin) beautiful.

Meiko
(Japanese) flower bud.

Meinwen
(Welsh) slender and fair-haired

friend.

Meira
(Hebrew) light.

Melanie
(Greek) dark-haired.

Melantha
(Greek) dark flower.

Melba
(Greek) soft; (Ir) mill stream; (Lat)
mallow flower.

Mele/Melle
(Hawaiian) poem; song.

Melecent/Millicent
(Greek) honeybee; (Ger) strength.
A form of Melissa.

Meleni
(Tongan) melon.

Melesse
(Ethiopian) eternal.

Melia
(Hawaiian) flower.

Melina
(Greek) song; (Lat) canary yellow;
gentle; sweet; honeybee. A form
of Melinda.

Meliora
(Latin) better.

Melisandre
(Greek/German/French)
determined; strength; strong
worker. A form of Millicent.

Melody
(Greek) song.

Melore
(Greek) golden apple.

Melosa
(Spanish) honeybee song. A
combination of Melissa and
Melody.

Melrose
(Greek/Latin/English) mill rose;
sweet rose. A combination of
Mel and Rose.

Mena
(German/Dutch) strength.

*Mercer
(English/French) merchant.

Merissa
(Latin) from the sea. A form

of Marissa.

Mesha
(Hindi) born under the sign of
Aries.

Messina
(Latin) middle child; harvest.

Mhairie
(Scottish/Hebrew) sea of bitterness;
lady of the sea. A form of Mary.

Mia
(Italian) mine.

Micaela
(Hebrew) who is like God. A feminine
form of Michael.

Micah/Mica
(Hebrew) who is like God. A short
form of Michaela and a feminine
form of Mike/Michael.

Michelle
(Hebrew/French) who is like God.
A feminine form of Michael.

Michonne/Mishone
(English/Irish/American) my God
is gracious. A combination of My
and Shawn.

Mieko
(Japanese) prosperous.

Miette
(French/English) little and sweet.

Mignon
(French) graceful and delicate.

Mignonette
(French/English) little flower;
graceful flower.

*Mika
(Omaha-Ponca/Osage) raccoon;
(Jap) new moon.

*Miki
(Japanese) three trees growing
together; (Haw) quick.

Mila/*Milan
(Slavic) loved by the people; (Ital)
from Milan.

Milena
(German) mild.

Milia
(German) hard working.

Mililani
(Hawaiian) heavenly caresses.

Millicent

(German) strong worker.

Milly/Millie
(German) hard working; (Heb)
labour of God. A form of Amelia.

Mima
(Wiradjuri) star; (Burm) woman.

Mimi
(Italian) my, my; (Fren) strong
willed; sea of bitterness; lady of
the sea. A form of Mary and a
French form of Miriam.

Mina
(Native American) fruit.

Minette
(French) faithful defender; (Eng) my
little one.

Minna/Mina
(German) love; determined and
little guardian; (Arab) wish;
(Eng) little; (Nat/Amer) first born
daughter. A short form of
Wilhelmina.

Minya
(Osage) eldest sister.

***Mio**
(Japanese) strength three times over.

Mira
(Latin) spectacular and beautiful.
A short form of names staring
with 'Mira' e.g. Mirabel.

Mirabel
(Latin) spectacular and beautiful.

Miranda
(Latin) worthy of admiration. A
form of Amanda.

Miri
(Hebrew/Gypsy) sea of bitterness;
lady of the sea. A form of Mary.

Missandei
(Old English/Greek) Young woman
who is strong and courageous.
A combination of Missy and Andy.

Moana
(Hawaiian) ocean; (Tong) deep sea.

Moina
(Irish) gentle and soft; sweet, noble
angel; (Grk) solitary; (Arab) wish;
(Lat) advise; (O/Eng) month. A
form of Mona.

Moira
(Irish) great; (Heb/Grk) fate;
sea of bitterness; lady of the sea.
The Irish form of Mary.

Mollee/Mollie/Molly
(Hebrew) wish.

***Monet**
(Greek/French) solitary.

Monique
(Latin/French) advisor; (Grk) solitary.

***Monroe**
(Irish) red marsh; roe river.

Mora
(Spanish) blueberry.

Morela
(Polish) apricot.

Morena/Moreen
(Spanish/Old French) dark-haired
or complexioned; (Ir) great. A form
of Maureen.

***Morgan**
(Scottish) sea bright; of the sea.

Morgwen
(Welsh) great and dark-haired or
complexioned friend.

Moria/Moriah

(French) dark-complexioned
or haired; (Heb) God is my teacher;
sea of bitterness; of the sea.
A form of Mariah/Mary.

*Morrin
(Irish) long-haired.

Mya
(Burmese) emerald.

Myla
(English) merciful.

Myra
(English) merciful.

Myrcella
(Old French/Italian) she is a
free and soft song; (Lat) scented
oil; wonderful; (Grk) plenty;
(Heb) to weep. A combination
of Myra and Cella.

N

Nadia
(Russian) hope.

Nadie
(Blackfoot) wisdom.

Naeva
(French/Hebrew) living. A

form of Eve.

Nairi
(Armenian) from the canyon
land.

Nairne
(Scottish) alder tree river.

Nakeita
(Russian/Greek) victory of the
people. A form of Nicole and the
feminine form of Nicholas.

Nakia
(Greek) victory of the people. A
form of Nicole and the feminine
form of Nicholas.

Nalani
(Hawaiian) calm heavens.

Nanetta/Nanette
(French/English) little and
graceful. A form of Annetta.

Narelle
(Aboriginal) light; woman from
the sea.

*Nari
(Japanese) thunder bolt.

Natalia/Natalie
(Latin) born on Christmas Day;
nativity.

Natania
(Russian) fairy queen; born on

Christmas Day; (Heb) gift of
God. A feminine form
of Nathaniel.

Natasha
(Latin/Russian) born on Christmas
Day; nativity. A form of Natalie.

*Natoma
(Native American) beautiful.

*Neige
(French) snow.

Nellie/*Nelly
(Greek) light; (Lat) yellow; horn;
the cornel tree. A short form
of Cornelia and a feminine form
of Cornelius.

Neola
(Greek) youthful.

*Neoma
(Greek) new moon.

Nerida
(Aboriginal) blossom; red
water lily.

Nerina
(Latin) black.

Nerine
(Greek) sea fairy.

Nerys
(Welsh) lady.

*Neva
(Spanish) white.

*Neve
(Hebrew) living. A form of
Eve.

Nevina
(Irish) the saint worshipper.

Ngaire
(Māori/Polynesian) family.

Niamh
(Irish) radiant; golden haired.

*Nic/*Nick/*Nicki/
Nickie/*Nicky
(Greek/English/Australian) victory

of the people. A short form of
Nicole/Nicole.

Nicola/Nicole
(Greek) victory of the people. A
feminine form of Nicholas.

Nicolina/Nicoline
(Greek/French) victory of the people.
A form of Nicole and the feminine
form of Nicholas.

Niesha
(Scandinavian) friendly fairy;
(Swah) life. A form of Keisha.

*Nika/*Nikah
(Russian) belonging to God.

Nikita
(Greek/Russian) victory of the
people. A form of Nicole and
the feminine form of Nicholas.

*Nila/Nile
(Latin) from the River Nile in Egypt.

Nima
(Hebrew) thread; (Arab) blessed.

Nina
(Spanish) girl; graceful. The
Russian form of Ann.

Ninette
(French) little.

Nioka
(Aboriginal) green grass.

Niree/Nyree
(Aboriginal) family; flax plant.

Nissa
(Scandinavian) friendly fairy;
(Heb) sign.

*Nita
(Choctaw) bear.

Noel/Noell/Noella/

Noelle/Noele
(Latin/French) born at
Christmas time. A feminine
form of Noel.

Nola
(Latin) small bell; noble; (Scot)
white-shouldered.

Novella
(Latin) newcomer; (Eng) small
novel.

*Novia
(Latin) youth; (Lat) new; (Span)
sweetheart.

Nuala
(Irish) fair shouldered.

*Nya/*Nyah
(Aboriginal) river bend.

Nyoko
(Japanese) gem.

Nyree
(Māori) sea.

Nyssa
(Greek) beginning; (Lat)
ambitious.

Obelia
(Greek) strength.

Octavia
(Latin) eighth born. A feminine
form of Octavius.

Odele/Odelle
(French) she is like a melody or
song.

Odelette
(French/English) little melody or
song.

Odelia
(Hebrew) praise to God; (Scand)
wealthy; little; (O/Eng) one who
resides in the valley. A feminine
form of Odell.

Odina
(Algonquin) mountain (Scand)
ruler. A feminine form of Odin.

Ohanna/Ohannah
(Hebrew) God is gracious. A form
of Hannah/Joanna.

Okalani
(Hawaiian) sent from heaven.

Ola
(Scandinavian) ancestral relic;
(Haw) life; well-being; (Nig)
precious.

Olalla
(Greek) speaking sweetly.

Olanthe
(Shawnee) beautiful.

*Oleander
(English/American) oleander tree.

Oleath/Oleatha
(English/Scandinavian) light;
(Grk) truth. A form of Alethea.

Olenna
(Russian) light. A form of Helena.

Olesia
(Polish) protector of humankind.

Olethea
(Greek/Latin) truth. A form of
Alethea.

Oliana
(Hawaiian) evergreen in flower;
flowering oleander tree.

*Olien
(Russian) deer.

Olienka
(Russian) holy.

Olina
(Hawaiian) happy.

Olinda
(Hawaiian/Latin) fragrant;
(span) pretty. A form of Linda.

Olisa
(Ibo) God-like.

Olive
(Latin) olive tree; peace.

Olivia
(Latin) olive tree; peace; (Scand)
holy.

Ona
(Latin/Scottish) unity; (Lith)
graceful; (Grk) donkey.

Onawa/Onowa
(Native American) wide-awake
girl.

Onora
(English) trustworthy. A form
of Honest/Honesta.

Oona
(Irish) lamb.

Opal/Opalina
(Sanskrit/Australian) precious
jewel; fire.

Ophelia
(Greek) wisdom; immortality.

Oriana
(Latin) golden light; (Heb)
graceful golden light. A combination
of Oriel and Anna.

Orina
(Greek/Russian) peaceful.

Orla
(Irish) golden.

Orlena
(Latin) golden.

Orlenda
(Russian) eagle.

Orli
(Hebrew) light.

Orna
(Irish) pale olive colour;
(Lat) decorated.

Osanna
(Latin) prayer; merciful.

Ottavia
(Italian) eighth born. A feminine
form of Octavius.

P

*Paige/*Page
(Old English) young child; intern; attendant.

Palmira
(Greek/Latin) land where palm trees grow; born on Palm Sunday, the Sunday before Easter. A feminine form of Palmiro.

Paloma
(Spanish/Latin) dove.

Parice
(Old French/Irish) ancient tribe that settled in France; from Paris France. A form of Paris and feminine form of Patrick.

*Paris
(Old French/Irish) ancient tribe that settled in France; from Paris France. A form of Patrice and Patrick.

*Pascha
(Hebrew) born at Easter time.

*Payton
(Old English) the warrior's town; the toll collector's town; (Ir) born of nobility. The Irish form of Patricia and a form of Peyton.

Pearl/Pearle
(Latin/English) pearl; pear-shaped.

Penelope
(Greek) weaver.

Penina
(Hebrew) pearl; coral.

Penny/Pene/Pennie
(Greek) weaver. A short form of Penelope.

Peony
(Greek) God of healing; giver of praise; a flower.

Perdita
(Latin) lost.

Perette
(French/English) little rock. A

feminine form of Peter.

Petrina
(Greek) steadfast; pure; rock. A
form of Katrina and a feminine
form of Peter.

*Peyton
(Old English) the warrior's town;
the toll collector's town; (Ir) born
of nobility. The Irish form of
Patricia and a form of Payton.

Phebe
(Greek) she shines brilliantly.
An Italian form of Phoebe.

Phedra
(Greek) bright.

Phelia
(Greek) immortal wisdom.

Philana
(Greek) one who loves horses.
A feminine form of Philip.

Philomela
(Greek) lover of songs.

Philomena
(Greek/Italian) one who loves horses;
she is loved; love song.

Phoebe
(Greek) she shines brilliantly.

Pia
(Latin/Italian) devout.

Pierette
(French) little and steadfast;
(Grk/Fren) little rock. A feminine
form of Pierre/Peter.

*Piper
(Old English) pipe player.

Pippa

(Greek) lover of horses. A
feminine form of Philip.

Pippi
(French) rosy cheeked.

Poeta
(Italian) poetry.

Polly
(Hebrew) sea of bitterness; lady
of the sea. A form of Mary.

*Poloma
(Native American) bow.

Poppy
(Latin/English) the poppy flower.

Portia
(Latin) offering; sweet fortified
wine; the left side; (O/Eng)
from the town by the
shipping wharf.

Preya
(Latin/English) prayer; (Hind)
beloved; sweet natured.

Primrose
(English/Scottish) delicate rose;
the primrose flower.

Priya
(Hindi) beloved; sweet natured.

Prudence/Prue
(Latin) foresight.

(Old English) quiet.

Quenby
(Swedish) woman; (Dan) home.

Quenna
(English) queen.

Quiana
(Hebrew) graceful. A form of
Anna.

*Quinby
(Scandinavian) the estate of
the queen.

*Quincy
(Latin) fifth born.

Quinella
(Latin) fifth born; (Eng) the
queen's lawn.

*Quinn
(Irish) the advisor's descendant;
(Eng) queen.

Quinta
(Latin) fifth born. A feminine
form of Quentin.

Quintana
(Latin) fifth born; (Eng) the
queen's lawn; (Heb/Eng) graceful
queen. A combination of Queen
and Anna.

Quintessa
(Latin) essence.

Quintina
(Latin/English) small fifth born child.

Q

Quella

R

Rachel
(Hebrew) ewe lamb.

Racquel
(Hebrew/French) ewe lamb. A
form of Rachel.

Raidah
(Arabic) leader.

*Rain
(English) precipitation.

Raina/Raine
(German/English) powerful
ruler; wisdom. A form of Regina.

Rainell
(English/French) she is the rain.

Raissa
(Old French) thinker; believer.

Ramia
(African) teller of fortunes.

Rana
(Scandinavian) catcher; (Sans)
royal; (Arab) gaze; (Span) frog.

*Ranait
(Irish) graceful.

Rane
(Scandinavian) queen.

Rani
(Sanskrit) queen; (Heb) joyous.

Rania
(Hindi) queen.

Ranita
(Hebrew) song of joy.

Raphaela
(Hebrew) God has healed. A
feminine form of Raphael.

Raquel/Raquelle
(Hebrew/Spanish) ewe lamb.
The Spanish form of Rachel.

Rasia
(Greek) rose.

Raven
(Old English) black bird;
black-haired.

Raya
(Hebrew) friend.

Rayna
(Hebrew) pure; (Scand) mighty.

Reanna
(German/English) mighty;
(Wel/Heb) graceful sorceress;
(Heb) graceful. A combination
of Rhiannon and Anna.

Rebecca
(Hebrew) bound; faithful.

*Reece
(Welsh) enthusiastic.

Reena
(Greek) peaceful.

*Regan
(Irish/Scottish/Latin) queenly;
regal.

*Rei
(Japanese) polite.

*Reiko
(Japanese) grateful.

Reina
(Spanish) queen. A form of Raina.

*Remy/*Remi
(French/English) raven; from
the champagne town Rheims.

Rena
(Hebrew) joyful song; A short
form of Irene/Irena.
Rene/*Renè/*Renee/

*Renèe
(French) reborn. A feminine
form of Rene.

Renita
(Latin) rebel.

*Renni
(Hebrew) song; (Fren) reborn.
A short form of Renee.

*Renny
(Irish) prosperous; small and strong.
A short form of names starting with
'Ren' e.g. Renee.

*Reva
(Latin) renewed strength; (Heb)
rain.

*Revaya
(Hebrew) satisfaction.

Rhea
(Greek) flowing stream; protector;
mother of all the Greek Gods.

Rhedyn
(Welsh) fern.

Rhian/Rhiana
(Welsh) sorceress; wisdom. A short
form of Rhiannon.

Rhiannon

(Welsh) sorceress; wisdom.

*Rhody
(Greek) rose.

*Ria
(Spanish) small river.

Riana
(Irish) virtue and strength.

Riane
(Irish/Scottish) little queen. A
feminine form of Ryan.

*Riley/*Ryley
(Irish/Scottish) valiant; war-like;
courageous; (O/Eng) rye meadow.

Riona
(Irish) queen.

*Riva
(French) stream.

*River
(Latin/French/English) large
stream.

*Rivkah
(French) shore.

*Robin/*Robyn
(Old English) the robin bird;
bright and famous; (O/Eng)
bright flame. A form of Roberta
and a feminine form of Robert.

Rochelle
(Old French) she is little like a
rock.

Rohana
(Hindi) sandalwood.

Roisin
(Latin/Irish) rose.

*Roma/Rome
(Italian) from Rome.

*Romain/*Romaine/*Rome
(French) from Rome.

*Romia
(Hebrew) highly praised.

*Romy
(French) from Rome. A short
form of Romaine.

Rona
(Irish) seal; (Heb) song of joy;
(Scand) powerful. A feminine
form of Ronald.

Ros/Roz
(Latin) rose.

Rosa
(Latin) rose.

Rosabelle/Rosabella
(Latin/Italian) beautiful rose.
A combination of Rose and
Belle/Bella.

Rosalee/Rosaleigh
(Latin/Old English) rose
meadow.

Rosalind
(Latin/Irish) little rose; (Span)
pretty rose; (O/Ger) horse.

Rosanna/Rosanne
(Latin/Old English) graceful rose.
A combination of Rose and Ann.

Rosee/Rosie/Rosey/Rosy
(Latin/English) little rose. A short
form of names starting with 'Rose'
e.g. Rosemary.

Roselani
(Latin/English/Hawaiian)
heavenly rose.

Rosemary
(Latin) the rosemary herb;
(Lat/Heb) wished for; bitter
rose; remembrance. A
combination of Rose and
Mary.

Rosetta
(Latin/English) little rose.

Rosina
(Latin/English) rose.

Rosita
(Latin/Spanish) rose.

Roslind
(Old French) little red-haired one;
rose. A feminine form of Roslin.

Rossalyn
(Latin/English/Scottish) cape
with a headland meadow;
(Lat/O/Eng) rose pool.

Rouge
(French) blushing; red.

*Rowan
(Scandinavian) red berry tree;
(Scott/Eng) rowan tree; (Eng)
famous friend; (Ir) little red-haired
one; (O/Nrs) mountain ash tree.

Roxanna/Roxanne
(Persian) sunrise.

Roza
(Latin/Slavic) rose.

Rozelle/Rozella
(Latin/Greek/French) she is a
rose.

Rozena
(Latin/Greek/Native American)
rose blossom.

Ruana
(Hindi) musical instrument.

Ruby
(Old French) ruby; (Lat) red.

Rumer
(Gypsy) gypsy.

*Rusty
(English) red-haired.

Ruth
(Hebrew) kindhearted; vision
of beauty; (O/Eng)
compassionate.

*Ryann/*Ryanna
(Irish) little and graceful queen;
regal. A feminine form of Ryan.

*Rylee/*Ryleigh/*Ryley
(Irish) courageous; (O/Eng)
rye meadow.

S

Sabina
(Latin) the Sabine, an ancient
people of Italy.

*Sable
(English) soft fur.

Sabrina
(Latin) boundary; (Heb)
seventh daughter; promise;
(Eng) princess.

*Sacha
(Greek) defender of humankind.
A form of Alexandra and
Alexander.

*Sachi
(Japanese) bringer of joy.

Sada
(Old English) seed.

Sade
(Hebrew) princess; lady. A
form of Sara.

Sadie
(Hebrew) princess; lady. A
form of Sara.

Sadira
(Persian) lily; (Arab) star.

Saffi

(Danish) wisdom.

Saffron
(Arabic) yellow or orange
colour; herb.

Safiya
(Arabic) pure; best friend.

*Sage
(Latin) healthy; wise; herb.

Sakara
(Hindi) sweet.

*Sakuna
(Native American) bird.

Sakura
(Japanese) cherry blossom;
wealthy.

*Sala
(Hindi) sacred tree.

Salali
(Cherokee) squirrel.

Salama
(Arabic) peace.

Salena
(Latin) salty; (Eng) princess.
A form of Sally.

Salima
(Arabic) safe.

Salina
(French) solemn.

Sally
(Hebrew) princess; lady.

Salma
(Swahili) safe.

Salome
(Hebrew) peace.

Salwa
(Arabic) bringer of comfort.

*Sam/*Sami/Sammi/
Sammie/*Sammy
(Hebrew) asked of God; heard
of God. A short form of names
starting with 'Sam' e.g. Samantha
and Samuel.

Samala
(Hebrew) asked of God; heard
of God.

Samantha
Aramaic) one who listens; (Heb)
asked of God; heard of God.

*Samar
(Arabic) night talker.

Samara
(Hebrew) guarded and ruled by
God.

Samaria/Samariah
(Hebrew) keeper, watcher; thorn.

*Sami
(Hebrew) highly praised. A native
people of Norway, Sweden, Finland
and Russia.

Samia
(Arabic) one who understands.

Samina
(Hindi) joy; (Eng/Heb) asked of
God; heard of God; little Sam.

Samira
(Arabic) entertainer.

*Samya
(Hebrew) rising.

73

Sana
(Hebrew) lily.

Sanchia/Sancia
(Latin) saintly; holy and pure.

*Sandy/Sandi/Sandie
(Greek) defender of humankind.
A short form of Alexandra/
Cassandra.

Sanjana
(Sanskrit) conscience, knowing
right from wrong.

Sanne
(Hebrew/Dutch) lily flower.

Sansa
(Sanskrit) charm; praised.

Sansana
(Hebrew) palm tree leaf.

Santina
(Spanish) little saint.

Sanya
(Sanskrit) born on a
Saturday.

Sara/Sarah
(Hebrew) princess; lady.

Saranna
(Hebrew) graceful princess;
graceful lady.

Saree/Sari
(Hebrew) princess; lady. A form
of Sara.

Sarina
(Hebrew/Arabic) princess; lady.
A form of Sara.

Saril/Sarila
(Turkish) waterfall.

Sarita
(Hebrew/Arabic) princess; lady.
A form of Sara.

Saronna
(Hebrew) princess of the plain;
his song; lady of the desert. A

combination of Sara and Sharon.

Sarotte
(Hebrew/French/Arabic) princess;
lady. A form of Sara.

*Sasha/*Sacha
(Greek/Russian) defender of
humankind. A form of Alexandra/
Sandra.

Satara
(Hebrew/Arabic/Irish) princess
from the rocky hill; lady from the
rocky hill.

Satoria
(Japanese) bird.

Saundra
(Greek/English) defender of
humankind. A form of Sandra/
Alexandra.

Saura
(Hindi) worshiper of the sun.

Savanna/Savannah
(Latin) open grassland.

Savina
(Latin) Sabine, an ancient people
of Italy.

Scarlet/Scarlett
(Middle English) a brilliant red
colour.

*Schuyler/*Skyler
(Dutch) shield; scholar.

*Sean/Seana

(Hebrew/Irish) God is gracious.

Seema
(Greek) symbol, sign.

*Seiko
(Japanese) accomplished.

Seini
(Polynesian) God is gracious.

Seirian/Seiriol
(Welsh) sparkling.

Seki
(Japanese) wonderful.

Sela
(Hebrew) stone.

Selena/Selene/Selina/Seline
(Latin/Greek) moon; heavenly. A
form of Celina/Celine.

Selma
(Scandinavian) divinely guarded;
(Arab) secure; (Ir) fair haired; (Heb)
peace. A feminine form of
Solomon.

Semira
(Hebrew) tall as the heavens.

Sen
(Japanese) magical forest fairy.

Sena
(Greek) welcomed. A form of
Xenia.

*Seon/Seona
(Hebrew/Scottish) God is gracious.
The Scottish form of Jane.

Seonaid
(Hebrew/Scottish) God is gracious.
The Scottish form of Jane.

Serah

(Hebrew) to pour; princess. A
form of Sarah.

Seraphina
(Spanish/Italian) the highest order
of the angels; (Heb) beloved. A
feminine form of Serafino.

Serena/Serene/Serina/
Serenity
(Latin) tranquil.

Serica
(Greek) silky.

Sevilla/*Seville
(French) willow tree village; from
Saville; prophet; (Fren) willow tree
town. The Spanish form of Sibyl.

*Shae/*Shay/*Shaye
(Irish) fairy palace. A form of Shea.

Shaelea/Shaleigh/Shaylee
(Irish/Old English) fairy palace in
the meadow. A form of Shea.

Shaelyn/Shaylin
(Irish/Welsh) pool by the fairy
palace. A form of Shea.

Shafira
(Swahili) distinguished.

*Shahar
(Arabic) born on a moonlit night.

Shaila
(Hindi) small mountain.

Shaina/Shaine/Shana/
Shayna/Shayne
(Hebrew/Irish) beautiful;
God is gracious. A feminine
form of Shane.

Shakeia/Shakia/Shikkia/
Shakkiah

(Blackfoot) unknown; (Afr)
beginning of the season. A
form of Kia.

Shakira
(Arabic) thankful.

Shalana
(Irish/Hawaiian) harmony; peace;
awakening; fair and beautiful; bright

and cheerful. A form of Alanna and
a feminine form of Alan.

Shaleah
(Irish/English) fairy palace in the
meadow. A form of Shea.

Shelena
(Norwegian) famous and
distinguished.

Shalisa
(Hebrew) oath to God; A form of
Lisa.

Shalona
(Middle English) lion-like; solitary.
A form of Lona.

Shalyn
(Welsh) shady pool; (Eng/Wel)
fairy palace by the pool.

Shamara
(Arabic) warrior.

Shameena
(Hindi) beautiful.

Shameka
(Hebrew) who is like God. A
feminine form of Mike/Michael.

Shamica
(Hebrew/American) who is like God.
A feminine form of Mike/Michael.

Shamika
(Native American) wise raccoon.

Shamira
(Latin) wonderful; (Span) to gaze.

Shammara
(Arabic) warrior.

Shana/Shanae
(Hebrew) God is gracious. A
feminine form of Shane.

Shanasa
(Hindi) wish.

Shanda
(Sanskrit) great Goddess.

Shaina/Shayna/Shane/
Shayne
(Irish) God is gracious.

Shaneka/Shanika
(Russian) belonging to God.

Shanelle
(French/English) from the strait.
A form of Chanel.

Shaneta
(Hebrew) plant.

Shani/Shanea
(American) marvellous; (Heb)
red.

Shania
(Ojibway) I'm on my way.

Shanice
(Hebrew) God is gracious. A
form of Janice.

*Shanie/*Shany
(Hebrew) beautiful; (It) God is
gracious. A feminine form of Shane.

Shanisa
(Hebrew) God is gracious; sign;
(Scand) friendly fairy. A combination
of Shane and Nissa.

*Shanley
(Irish) child of the hero; (Heb/Eng)
God's gracious meadow.

Shanna
(Irish) slow water; (Heb) God is
gracious. A feminine form of Shane.

*Shannon
(Irish) small, wise; slow stream.

Shantelle
(French) she is a song. A form of
Chantal.

Shantille
(French) fine and delicate; lace.
A form of Chantilly.

Sharice
(French) joyful song.

*Shaun/Shauna
(Irish) God is gracious. The Irish
form of Jane.

Shavonne/Shavaughn
(Irish) God is gracious. A form of
Siobhain/Siobhan.

*Shay/*Shae
(Irish) fairy palace.

Shayla
(Irish) fairy palace; (Hind) throne.

Shayna/*Shayne
(Hebrew) beautiful fairy palace;
(Ir) God is gracious. A feminine
form of Shane.

*Shea
(Irish) fairy palace; majestic.

Sheina
(Hebrew) gift from God; God is

gracious. A form of Shane.

*Shelby
(Old English) estate by the sea.

Shelley/Shelly
(Old English) seashell meadow. A
short of Michelle/Roshelle.

Shena
(Irish) God has favoured; God is
gracious. A feminine form of Sean

and the Irish form of Jane.

Shenoa
(Irish/Latin/French) she is unity,
she is one.

Sherelle
(French) she is the beloved.

*Sheriden/*Sheridan
(Irish) wild; wild butterfly; (O/Eng)
sheep valley; shire valley.

Sherilyn
(Old English/Welsh) beloved pool.
A combination of Sheryl and Lyn.

*Shiloh
(Hebrew) sent.

Shiona
(Lithuanian) graceful.

Shonda
(Irish) God is gracious. A form
of Shona and a feminine form of
Sean/Shaun/Shane.

Shoshana
(Hebrew) lily. A form of Susanna.

Shu
(Chinese) kind and gentle.

Shumana
(Native American) rattle snake
girl. A form of Chumana.

*Shyla
(English) shy.

Sia
(Persian) she brings joy.

Siaina
(Tongan) from China.

Siale
(Tongan) flowering bush.

Sialea
(Navajo) little blue bird.

Sialea-Lea
(Navajo) little blue bird
who is a good dreamer.

Sianna/Siannah
(Irish) health; God is gracious.
A feminine form of Sean.

Siany
(Irish) health; God is gracious. A
feminine form of Sean.

Sibena
(Greek) alluring, Siren.

Sidonia
(Greek) cloth of fine linen;
(Phoe) enchantress.

Sienna/Siennah/Siena
(Irish) health; God is gracious. A
feminine form of Sean.

Signy
(Scandinavian) victory.

Sigourney
(English) victorious conqueror; (Heb)
lily. A form of Susan.

Sigrid
(Old Norse/German) beautiful
victory.

Silvia/Sylvia/Sylvie
(Latin) silver; woods.

Sina
(Irish) God is gracious.

Sindy/Cindy/Cindee
(French) little ashes; moon. A short
form of Cinderella/Cynthia.

Sinead
(Irish) God is gracious. The Irish
form of Jane.

Siobhain/Siobhan
(Irish) God is gracious. The Irish
form of Jane.

*Sion/Syon
(Hebrew) highly praised.

Sirena
(Greek) alluring, Siren.

Sirri/Siri
(Finnish) princess. The Finnish
form of Sara.

*Sisika
(Native American) songbird.

Sivia
(Hebrew) deer.

*Sky/*Skye
(English) heavenly; (Dut) shelter.
A short form of Skyler.

*Skye/*Skyler
(Dutch) shelter; scholar.

*Sloan/*Sloane
(Scottish/Irish) warrior.

Sofia/Sofie
(Greek) wisdom.

*Sol
(Spanish/Norse/Latin) sun.

*Solace
(Latin) comfort in a time of
misery.

Solana
(Spanish) sunshine; (Lat) easterly

wind.

Solange
(French) sun angel; (Lat) alone;
(Fren) solemn, dignified.

Soleil
(French) sunflower.

Solita
(Latin) accustomed.

*Sommer
(Old English) summer; (Arab)
black.

*Sona
(Latin) noisy.

Sonel
(Hebrew) lily. A form of Susan.

Sonia
(Greek) wisdom. The
Scandinavian and Slavic
forms of Sophia.

Sooki
(Hebrew) lily.

Sopheary
(Cambodian) beautiful.

Sophia/Sophie
(Greek) wisdom.

Sora
(Native American) songbird
chirping.

Soraya

(Persian) princess.

Sorcha
(Irish) princess; bright. The Irish
form of Sara.

*Sorrell
(French) reddish/brown
coloured-hair.

*Soso
(Native American) chubby-
checked baby; pine nut
eating squirrel.

Stacey/Stacie/Stacia
(Greek) resurrection; springtime.
A short form of Anastasia.

*Star
(Old English) celestial body, star.

Starla
(Old English) celestial body, star.

Starlee/Starli/Starlie/
Starly
(Old English) star-filled meadow.

Stassie/Stassy
(Greek/Spanish/Russian)
resurrection; springtime. A short
form of Anastacia.

Stella
(Latin) star. A short for of Estella.

Stephanie/Stevana
(Greek) crowned. A feminine form
of Steven/Stephen.

Stevi/*Stevie/*Stevey/
*Stevy
(Greek/American) crowned.
A short form of Steven/Stephen
and a short form of Stephanie.

Stina
(German/Greek) Christian;
(Eng) little. A short form of names

ending in 'stina' e.g. Christina.

*Storm/Stormi/*Stormie/
*Stormy
(Old English) tempest.

Suke/Sukey
(Hebrew/Hawaiian) lily. A short
form of Susan.

Suki
(Moquelumnan) eagle-eyed;
(Jap) beloved.

Sula
(Icelandic) large sea bird.

Sulia
(Latin) youthful. A form of
Julia.

Suma
(Tanzanian) asked for.

Summerlea/Sommerlee
(Thai) beautiful flower;
(Eng/O/Eng) summer
meadow.

Sumatie
(Hindi) unity.

Sumi
(Japanese) elegant.

Sumiko
(Japanese) child of goodness;
beautiful child.

*Summer
(English) born during summertime.

*Sun
(Korean) obedient; (Eng) bright,
sun.

*Sun Hi
(Korean) happy and good.

*Sunee
(Thai) good; (Eng) sunny, happy.
A form of Sunny.

*Sunni/*Sunnie/*Sunny
(English) sunshine; happy;
(Nat/Amer) star. A feminine
form of Sonny.

Surata
(Pakistani) blessed happiness.

Suri
(Sanskrit) sun mother; (Heb)
princess; (Per) red rose;

(Armen) wealth; (Span) pointy nose.

Svetlana
(Russian/Slavic) star; light.

Sybella/Sybelle
(Greek/Italian/French) beautiful
prophet. A combination of Sybil
and Bella/Belle.

Sydella/Sydelle
(Hebrew) princess.

Sydney/Sidney
(Old French) from St Denis;
(Eng) wide; (Phoe) enchanter.

Sying
(Chinese) star.

Syke
(Greek) mulberry tree.

Sylvana/Sylvania
(Latin) woods.

Sylvia/Sylvie
(Latin) woods.

Syona
(Hindi) joy.

T

Tabina
(Arabic) follower of
Muhammad.

*Tacey
(English) peaceful; silence.

Tahnee
(Russian/Slavic) fairy queen;
(Eng) little.

*Tailor/*Taylor
(Old English) tailor; maker or
repairer of clothes. A form of
Taylor.

Taima
(English) tamer of animals.

*Tais
(Greek) bound together, bonded.

Taja
(Hindi) crown. A feminine form
of Taj.

Takara
(Japanese) precious treasure.

Takira
(Persian) sun; (Lat) light.

*Talasi
(Hopi) corn tassel.

*Tale
(Botswana) green; (Eng) story
maker.

Taleah
(Old English) tall tree meadow.

Talena
(Latin) temptress; (Nor) hard
working; (Heb) home.

Talia
(Greek) flowering; (Heb) gentle
dew drops from heaven.

*Taliesin
(Welsh) glowing brow.

Talisa/Talissa
(English/American) honeybee;
(Heb) joy. A form of Melissa
or Alyssa.

Talise/Talice
(Creek) beautiful water.

Talitha
(Hebrew) child; (Ara) woman.

*Tallara
(Aboriginal) rain.

*Tallis
(English/French) woods.

*Tallon/*Talon
(Latin/Middle English/
Old French) claw.

Tallulah
(Choctaw) leaping water.

*Tally
(Hebrew) child.

*Talma
(Native American) crash of
thunder.

*Talmah
(Hebrew) small hill.

*Talya
(Hebrew) little lamb.

*Tam
(Vietnamese) heart. A short form
of names starting with 'Tam' e.g.
Tammy.

*Tama
(Hebrew) palm tree; pigeon; (Jap)
polished jewel.

*Tamah
(Hebrew) a wonder.

Tamanna
(Hindi) desire.

*Tamar/Tamara
(Hebrew) palm tree; date fruit.

*Tamas/Tamassa
(Hindi) night; (Heb/Ara) twin.
A feminine form of Thomas.

Tamasina
(Aramaic) twin. A feminine form
of Thomas.

Tameka
(Hebrew) twin. A feminine form
of Thomas.

Tami

(Japanese) people.

Tamiko
(Japanese) the people's child.

Tamila
(Russian) dearest.

**Tammy/Tammi/
Tammie**
(Hebrew) perfection; palm tree;
date fruit.

Tamra
(Hebrew) palm tree; date fruit.
A form of Tamara.

Tamsin
(Hebrew/English/Scandinavian)

twin. A feminine form of Tamson.

*Tana
(Aboriginal) ceremony.

Tanah
(Slavic/Russian) fairy queen. A
form of Tania/Tanya.

Tanasha
(Slavic/Russian) fairy queen born
on Christmas Day. A combination
of Tanya and Natasha.

Tanay
(Hindi) daughter.

*Tandie/*Tandy
(Greek) immortal.

Taneya
(Russian/Slavic) fairy queen.

*Tani
(Japanese) valley; (Span) famous.

*Taniel
(Hebrew/Estonian) (Hebrew)
God is my judge; gift of God.
A form of Danielle or Daniel

and short form of Nathaniel.

Tannis
(Slavic) fairy queen.

Tansy
(English) the tansy herb; (Lat)
persistent; (Grk) immortal.

*Tao
(Chinese/Vietnamese) peach
flower child.

Tara
(Irish) rocky hill; (Ara) to carry;
(Arab) measure.

*Tari
(Irish) rocky hill. A form of
Tara.

*Tarne
(Scandinavian) mountain lake.

*Tarni
(Kaurna) sea water.

*Taryn
(Irish) peaceful and rocky hill.
A combination of Tara and
Erin.

Tashelle
(Hebrew) born on Christmas Day;

who is like God. A combination
of Michelle and Natasha.

*Tashi
(Hausa) bird flying.

*Tasma
(Hebrew/Aramaic) twin; (Slav)
born on Christmas Day. A
feminine form of Thomas and
the short form of Tasmin.

*Tasmin
(Hebrew/Aramaic) twin. A form of
Thomas.

*Tate
(Old English) cheerful;
(Native Amer) long talker;
(O/Eng) spirited; cheerful.

Tatiana
(Russian) fairy queen.

*Tatsu
(Japanese) dragon.

*Tatum
(Old English) from Tate's
homestead; cheerful; from the
spirited and cheerful one's
town; (Nat/Amer) long talker.

*Tavia
(Latin) eighth born. A form of
Octavia.

*Tavie
(Scottish/Hebrew/Aramaic)
twin; (Aram) good. A short
form of Tavish.

*Tawny/Tawnie
(English) light brown
complexioned; child; (Gyp) little.

*Taya
(Japanese) homestead in the
valley field.

*Taye
(English) tailor of clothes. A short
form of Taylor.

Taylea/Taylee/Tayleigh/
Tayley
(Old English) tall tree meadow.

*Taylor/Tayla/*Tailor
(Old English) tailor; maker or
repairer of clothes.

Téa
(Welsh) beautiful; (Ir) doe. A
short form of Teagan.

Teagan
(Welsh) beautiful; (Ir) doe.

*Teal/*Teale
(Middle English) sea green/
blue; duck.

Teanna
(Welsh/Hebrew) graceful
and beautiful. A combination
of Téaand Anna.

Tegan
(Irish) doe; (Wel) beautiful. A form
of Teagan.

Tegan Evvron
(Irish) beautiful doe; (Ir/Heb)
fruitful doe.

*Telae
(Tongan) fish.

Tempany
(Latin) storm. A form of Tempest.

*Tempest
(Latin) storm.

Tennille
(Irish/English) champion. A
feminine form of Neil.

Terrelle
(Greek/French) she is the harvester.

Tess
(Greek) harvester; fourth born. A
short form of Theresa.

Tessa
(Polish) loved by God.

*Tevy
(Cambodian) angel.

Thalia

(Greek) flourishing, flowering.

Thao
(Vietnamese) one who respects her parents.

Thea
(Greek) gift. A short form of Dorothea.

Theodora
(Greek) gift of God. A feminine form of Theodore.

Theophila
(Greek) beloved of God.

Theora
(Greek) watchful.

Theresa/Therese
(Greek) harvester.

Tia/Tiah
(Tongan) deer; (Egypt) princess.

Tiana/Tianna
(Russian) fairy queen; (Heb/Egypt) graceful princess. A short form of Tatiana.

Tiara
(Latin) jewelled crown.

*Tierney
(Scottish) grandchild of the chief.

Tiffany
(Greek) God appears to her.

Tilda
(German) powerful warrior.

Tilly
(German) strength through battle; (Grk) fortunate warrior. A short form of Matilda.

*Tira
(Hebrew) enclosure; (Hind) arrow.

Toinette
(Latin/French) priceless. A short form of Antoinette and a feminine form of Anthony.

*Tori/*Tory
(Scandinavian) Thor; thunder; (Jap) bird; (Lat) victory. A short form of Tori/Victoria.

Toriana
(Latin/Hebrew) graceful victory. A combination of Tori and Anna.

*Toshi
(Japanese) mirror reflection; she resembles her mother; year.

*Trinity
(Latin) group of three, triplet; the Father, the Son and the Holy Spirit.

Tristabella/Tristabelle
(Welsh/Italian) beautiful and loud; beautiful, bold knight; (Wel/Fren/Ital) beautiful.

Tristianna/Tristianne
(Welsh/Hebrew) graceful, beautiful and loud; graceful and bold knight; (Wel/Fren) sorrowful and graceful.

Trudy
(German) spear strength. A short form of Gertrude.

*Tu
(Chinese) jade stone.

*Tula
(Hindi) peace.

*Tully
(Irish/Scottish) one who lives
with the peace of God;
mighty people.

Twyla
(Old English) woven, double
thread.

*Tya
(Wemba-Wemba) earth.

Tyanna
(Latin/English) graceful.

Tyna
(Slavic/English) little.

*Tyne
(Old English) river.

U

Ualani
(Hawaiian) heavenly rain.

Udele/Udelle
(Old English) prosperous.

Ujana
(Breton) noble and excellent.

*Ula
(Irish) jewel of the sea; (O/Ger)
inheritor; (Span) wealthy.

Ulani

(Hawaiian) lighthearted;
heavenly.

Ulla
(Old French) to fill; (O/Nrs)
will; (Ger) willful; (Arab)
wisdom.

*Ulu
(Nigerian) second born.

Uma
(Sanskrit) peace; (Heb) nation;
(Hind) mother.

Una
(Hopi) remembering; memory;
(Ir) lamb; (Lat) one.

Undina/*Undine
(Latin) wave of water.

Unn
(Norwegian) she is loved.

Unna
(Icelandic/German) woman.

*Unnea
(Old Norse) linden or lime tree.

Ursula
(Latin) little bear.

V

Vailea
(Polynesian) talking water.

Vala
(Gothic/German) chosen.

Valencia
(Spanish) strength.

Valentia
(Latin) strength.

Valentina
(Latin) strength. A feminine
form of Valentine/Valentino/

Valentinus.

*Valentine
(Latin) strength.

Valera
(Latin/Russian) strength;
(O/Eng) valley. A form of Valerie.

Valeria
(Latin/Italian/German) strength;
(O/Eng) valley. A form of Valerie.

Valeska
(Slavic) glorious ruler. A feminine
form of Vladislav.

*Vallia
(Spanish) powerful protector.

Vallonia
(Latin) acorn.

Valonia
(Latin) strength; (Eng) valley.

A form of Valerie.

Valora
(Latin) strength and courage.

Vana
(Polynesian) sea urchin.

Vania
(Hebrew) God is gracious. A
feminine form of Ivan.

Vanja
(Scandinavian) God is gracious.

Vanka
(Hebrew/Russian) graceful.
The Russian form of Anne.

Vanna
(Old English) high.

Vanora
(Irish) white wave.

Vantrice
(Greek) harvester.

Vanya
(Hebrew/Russian) graceful. A
form of Anna.

Vara
(Norse) cautious.

*Varana
(Hindi) river.

Vardina
(Hebrew) rose.

*Vardis
(Hebrew) rose.

Varina
(Latin/Russian) stranger.
A form of Barbara.

*Varsha
(Hindi) rain.

Varvara
(Latin) stranger. A form of
Barbara.

*Varuna
(Russian) one who sees all.

Veanna
(Hebrew/American) graceful.
A form of Anna.

Veera
(Hindi) strength.

*Vega
(Latin) star constellation.

*Vela
(Latin) a star constellation in
the Milky Way.

Velinda
(Latin/American) honeybee. A
form of Melinda.

*Vellamo
(Finnish) rocking.

Velma
(German) determined guardian.
A short form of Vilhelmina.

Velvet
(Middle English) velvety; soft;
(Lat) fleece.

Venecia/Venetia
(Italian) from Venice, Italy; (Lat)
kind and merciful; bringer of
happiness.

*Venice
(Italian) from Venice, Italy;
(Lat) kind and merciful; she
brings happiness.

Vera
(Latin/Russian) faithful.

*Veradis
(Latin) faithful.

Verbena
(Latin) sacred branch.

Verda
(Persian) rose; (Lat) young.

*Verdi
(Latin) green like the
springtime.

Verena
(Swedish) sacred wisdom;

(O/Ger) defender; (Lat)
faithful.

Verina
(Latin) faithful.

Verity
(Latin) truthful.

Verla
(Latin) faith.

Vermona
(Latin) springtime.

Vernice
(Greek) one who brings victory;
(Ger) strong, brave little bear;
warrior. The feminine form of
Bernie/Bernard.

Verona
(Italian) truth; true to image. A form
of Veronica.

Veronica
(Latin) truth, true to image.

Verra
(Slavic) faith.

Vervain
(Old English) sacred.

Vesper/Vespera
(Latin) evening star.

Vesta
(Italian) Goddess of fire; (Lat)
Goddess of the home.

Veva
(Welsh) white wave; fair-haired.
A short form of Genevieve.

Vevay
(Irish) white wave; fair-haired.

Vevetta/Vevette
(French) fair-haired; white wave.

Vevila
(Irish) harmony.

Vevina
(Scottish) sweet lady.

Vi
(Latin/French) violet. A short

form of names starting with 'Vi'
e.g. Viola.

Vianca
(Spanish/Italian) white. A form
of Bianca.

Vianna/Vianne
(Latin/Old French/Hebrew)
graceful violet flower. A combination
of Violet and Anna/Anne.

*Vic/*Vica
(Hebrew/Hungarian) living. A
form of Eve. (Lat) victory.
A form of Victor/Victoria.

Victoria
(Latin) victory.

Victorine/Victorina
(Latin) victory.

Vida
(Hebrew) beloved. A form

of David.

*Vidal
(Latin) life.

Vidonia
(Portuguese) vine or branch.

*Vienna
(Hebrew/Latin) graceful;
from Vienna, Australia.

*Vikka
(Latin) victory. A short form
of Victoria/Victoria.

Vilhelmina
(German) determined
guardian. A form of
Wilhelmina.

Villette
(French) little village.

Vilma

(Dutch) willful. A feminine
form of William.

Vilmah
(Russian) protector.

Vina
(Spanish) vineyard.

Vinah
(Scottish) beloved. A feminine
form of David.

Vincentia
(Latin) conqueror. A feminine
form of Vincent.

Vinia
(Latin) grapes; wine.

Vinita
(Spanish) vineyard.

Vinna
(Spanish) vine.

Viola
(Latin) the violet flower;
(Ital) stringed musical
instrument.

Violani
(Latin/Hawaiian) heavenly
violet flower.

Violante
(Latin/Spanish) the violet
flower.

Violet
(Latin/Old French) the violet
flower; dark purple.

Vira
(Latin) blond-haired; (Ger)
closed; (Span) elf advisor.

Vita
(Latin) full of life; beloved. A
short form of Davita.

Vittoria
(Latin/Italian) victory. A
form of Victoria.

Viva
(Latin) full of life. A short form
of Vivien.

Viveca
(Scandinavian) full of life;
alert.

*Viv/*Vivian
(Latin) full of life.

*Voila
(French) behold.

*Volante
(Italian) flying.

Voleta
(Old French) flowing veil;
(O/Eng) little violet.

Vonda
(Irish/Hebrew) admired;
God is gracious. The Irish form
of Joanna or Siobhain.

Vondra
(Slavic) brave and courageous.

Vonna/Vonny
(French) archer; (Scand) yew
wood. A form of Yvonne.

Vye
(Netherlandic) wisdom.

*Waida
(German) warrior.

Waratah
(Aboriginal) red flower.

Whitney
(Old English) white island;
clear and white water.

Wila
(Hawaiian) faithful.

Willa
(German) willful.

*Willow
(English) willow tree.

Wilona
(German) willful guardian;
(Dut) willful.

Winnie
(English) peaceful and friendly;
(Wel) fair-haired; white. A short
form of names starting with 'Win'
e.g. Winifred.

Winola
(German/Welsh) gracious
and generous fair-haired friend.

Winona/Wynona
(Lakota) first born daughter.

*Winter/*Wynter
(English) born during wintertime.

Wira
(Latin/Polish) blond-haired;
(Ger) closed.

Wren/Wrena
(Old English) the wren bird.

Xanthe
(Greek) golden-haired; yellow.

Xanthia
(Greek) yellow-haired; yellow.

Xara
(Hebrew) princess. A form of
Sara.

*Xaverie
(Aramaic) bright.

Xaviera
(Arabic) bright; (Span) owner of
the new house. A feminine
form of Xavier.

*Xayvion
(Spanish/American) new home.

Xela
(French) mountain home.

*Xen/Zen
(Japanese) spiritual; (Chin) pure.

Xenia/Xena
(Greek) living; welcomed.

Xiang
(Chinese) fragrant.

*Ximena
(Hebrew/Spanish) hearing;
obeying. A feminine form
of Simon.

Xina
(English) little; (Grk)

welcomed.

Xirena
(Greek) mermaid; Siren.
A form of Sirena.

Xiu Mei
(Chinese) beautiful plum.

*Xuan
(Vietnamese) spring.

Xya
(Latin) grain; trembling;
(Ital) aunt. A form of Zia.

Xylia/Xylina/Xylona
(Greek) wood dweller.

*Yachi
(Japanese) good fortune.

*Yael
(Hebrew) mountain goat.

Yakira
(Hebrew) precious.

Yalena
(Greek/Russian) light. A form

of Helen.

Yamelia
(German) hard working. A
form of Amelia.

Yamilla
(Slavic) trader.

Yaminah
(Arabic) proper.

*Yamini
(Hindi) nighttime.

Yana
(Slavic/Hebrew) God is gracious.
A form of Jana and Anna.

*Yang
(Chinese) sun.

*Yani
(Aboriginal) peaceful.

*Yara
(Aboriginal) bird of the sea, seagull.

*Yaralla
(Aboriginal) camping area.

*Yardley
(Old English) enclosed
meadow.

Yarina
(Slavic/Greek) peaceful.

Yasmin/Yasmina/Yasmine/
Yasmyn/Yasmyna/Yasmyne
(Arabic) the jasmine flower. A
form of Jasmine.

*Yasu
(Japanese) tranquil.

*Ye
(French/Greek) kind; good.

A form of Agatha.

Yelena
(Latin) lily; (Lat/Russ) light. A
form of Helena.

Yemena
(Arabic) from Yemen.

Yemina
(Hebrew) little dove.

*Yen
(Chinese) desire; (Viet) calm.

Yenene
(Native American) shaman,
medicine woman.

*Yeo
(Korean) mildness.

Yesenia
(Latin) flower.

Yesima
(Hebrew) strength of the right hand.

Yetta
(Old English) she gives; little ruler

of the house. A short form of
Henrietta.

Yeva
(Greek/Ukrainian) good news
bringer; living. A form of Eve.

Ygritte
(French/Greek) archer's bow made

of pearl. A combination of Yvette
and Greta.

*Yilla
(Aboriginal) cicada.

*Yin
(Chinese) silver.

*Yoi
(Japanese) born in the evening.

Yoko
(Japanese) positive.

Yola
(Greek) the violet flower; purple.
A short form of Yolanda.

Yolanda
(Greek) the violet flower; purple.

Yordana
(Basque) descended.

*Yori
(Japanese) reliable.

*Yoshe
(Japanese) lovely.

*Yoshi
(Japanese) quiet.

Yoshiko
(Japanese) good.

Yovela
(Hebrew) rejoicing.

Ysabel
(Spanish) oath to God. A form
of Isabelle.

Ysanne
(Old Spanish) dedicated to God.

Yseult
(Irish) light complexioned.

*Yu
(Chinese) jade stone.

Yuana
(Hebrew/Spanish) God is gracious.

Yudelle

(Old English) prosperous. A
form of Udele.

Yudita
(Hebrew/Russian) praised.

Yula
(Russian) young.

*Yulan
(Chinese) jade; orchid.

Yulene
(Latin/Basque) youthful. A
form of Julia.

Yulia
(Latin/Russian) youthful. A
form of Julia.

Yuri
(Japanese) lily.

Yvanna
(Slavic) God is gracious. A form of Ivana.

Yvette
(French) young archer; archer's
bow; knight of the lion. A form
of Yvette and a feminine
form of Yves.

Yvonne
(French) young archer; archer's bow;
knight of the lion. A form of
Yvette and a feminine form of Yves.

Z

Zabrina
(Latin) boundary; (Heb) seventh
daughter; promise; (Eng) princess.
A form of Sabrina.

Zada

(Arabic) lucky.

Zafina/Zaffira
(Arabic) triumphant.

*Zahar
(Hebrew) dawn.

Zahavah
(Hebrew) gold.

Zahira
(Arabic) bright.

Zahra
(Arabic) white; (Swa) flower.

Zahrah
(Hebrew) princess. A form
of Sara.

Zaida
(Arabic) good fortune; growth;
hunter.

Zaidee
(Arabic) wealthy; (Heb) princess.
A form of Sadie.

Zainab
(Arabic) mother of the poor.

Zaira
(Arabic) dawn.

*Zakah
(Hebrew) pure.

*Zakia
(Swahili) intelligent;
(Arab) pure.

Zali
(Hebrew/Polish) princess. A form
of Sara.

*Zan
(Chinese) praised.

Zana

(Persian) woman.

Zanna
(Spanish) God is gracious; lily.
A form of Jane and an English
form of Susanna.

Zara/Zarah
(Arabic) dawning; (Heb) princess.
A form of Sara.

Zarina
(Hindi) gold.

Zarita
(Hebrew) princess. A form
of Sara.

Zasha
(Greek/Russian) defender of
humankind. A form of Sasha.

Zaza
(Hebrew) golden; swift.

Zea
(Latin) grain.

Zeborah
(Hebrew/American) honeybee.
A form of Deborah.

Zehira
(Hebrew) protected; guarded.

Zelda
(Yiddish) grey-haired.

Zelene
(English) sunshine; (Lat/Grk)
moon; heavenly. A form of
Selena/Seline.

Zelenka
(Slavic) little and innocent.

Zelia
(Greek) enthusiastic; (Span)
sunshine; (Lat) unseeing. A form
of Cecelia.

Zelkova
(Russian) elm tree.

Zella
(Hebrew) shelter.

Zelmah
(Turkish) protected.

Zemira
(Hebrew) song.

*Zen
(Japanese) spiritual; (Chin) pure.

Zena
(Persian) woman; (Grk)
welcomed.

Zenda
(Persian) sacred.

Zenia
(Greek) enthusiastic;
welcomed.

Zephania
(Hebrew) crown. A form of
Stephanie and a feminine
form of Steven/Stephen.

Zephira
(Hebrew) morning.

Zephrine
(Hebrew/English) breeze.

Zera
(Latin) seeds.

Zerlina
(Hebrew/Latin) beautiful
dawn.

*Zerrin
(Turkish) golden.

Zeta
(Hebrew) olive.

Zetta
(Portuguese) rose.

*Zeva
(Greek) sword; (Heb) wolf.

Zia
(Hebrew) trembling; (Lat) grain;
(Ital) aunt.

Zila
(Hebrew) shade.

Zilia
(Italian) fair-haired; white wave.
A form of Genevieve.

Zillah
(Hebrew) shadow.

Zina
(African) name; (Heb) plenty.

Zinnia
(Latin) the zinnia flower.

Ziva
(Hebrew) light. The Slavic Goddess
of light.

Zizi
(Russian) her father's ornament.

Zoe
(Greek) life.

Zoia
(Russian) life. A form of Zoe.

Zolah
(Italian) mound of earth.

Zophie
(Greek/Bohemian) wisdom. A
form of Sophie.

Zora/Zorah

(Slavic) beautiful, golden dawn.

Zosima
(Greek) lively; wealthy.

Zoya
(Greek/Slavic) life. A form of
Zoe.

Zsa
(Hebrew/Hungarian) lily. A form
of Susan.

*Zuni
(Native American) the name of a
Native American Nation.

Zuri
(Swahili) beautiful; (Basq)
white-complexioned.

Zusa
(Hebrew/Slavic/Polish) lily.
A form of Susan.

BOY NAMES

A

Abban
(Latin) white.

Abe
(Hebrew) high father. A short form
of Abraham.

Abel
(Hebrew) breath; mourning, son;
noble; ambitious. A short form
of Abelard.

Abelard
(Old German) noble; ambitious.

Abidan
(Hebrew) father of judgment.

Abraham/Abram
(Hebrew) high father.

Achaicus
(Hebrew) sad.

Achim
(Hebrew) resurrection.

*Ackerley
(English) oak tree meadow.

*Acton
(Old English) acorn tree town;
oak tree town.

*Adair
(Scottish) oak tree.

Adam
(Hebrew) red earth; man.

Adamson
(Hebrew/Old English) son of

Adam; red earth; man.

Adan/Addan
(Arabic) pleasure; foundation.

Addison
(Old English) son of Adam; son

of the red earth; son of man.

*Aden
(Irish) fiery.

*Adlee/Adley
(Hebrew) righteous; just.

Adrian
(Greek) dark; dark-haired.

Adriel
(Hebrew) God's kingdom;
(Nat/Amer) beaver; skillful
worker.

Adwin
(Ghanaian) creative.

Aegir
(Old Norse) sea God.

*Afton
(English) from Afton in
England.

Agrey
(Latin) open field; grey.

Aidan
(Irish) small and fiery.

Aiken
(Old English) beautiful oak.

Aimon
(French) house.

*Ain
(Scottish) belonging to oneself;
(Ir) joy; fire. A short form of
names beginning with 'Ain'
e.g. Ainsley

*Ainslee/*Ainsleigh/
*Ainsley
(Scottish) open country meadow;
strong and courageous meadow;
(O/Eng) meadow clearing.

Ajax

(Greek) eagle.

*Ajay
(Punjabi) victorious.

*Akira
(Japanese) intelligent.

Akmal
(Arabic) perfection.

Alain
(Irish/French) harmony; peace;
fair and beautiful; bright and
cheerful. A masculine form of
Alanna and Alan.

*Alair
(Irish) joy.

*Alaire
(French) joy.

Alam
(Arabic) universe.

Alan
(Irish) harmony; peace; fair and
beautiful; bright and cheerful.
A masculine form of Alanna and a
form of Alan.

Alaric
(Old German) hard and noble
ruler; fierce; wolf ruler.

Alastair
(Greek) avenger.

Alben
(Latin) fair complexioned.

Albert
(German) noble, industrious,
bright and famous.

*Albie
(German/French) noble and bright.
A short form of names starting

with 'Albi' e.g. Albion.

Albin/Albion
(Scottish) white cliffs.

Alcander
(Greek) defender of humankind.
A form of Alexander.

*Alcott
(Old English) old cottage; alder
tree cottage.

*Aldan
(Old English) wise, old friend; helmet.

*Alder
(Old English) alder tree.

Alderidge
(Old English) ridge near the alder
tree farm.

Aldis
(Old French) old house.

Aldo
(Old German) old and wise.

Aldous
(Old German) old and wise;
(O/Eng) old house.

Aldred
(Old English) old and wise
advisor.

Aldrich
(Old German) old, wise and
powerful ruler; (Eng) wise advisor.

Aldwin
(Old English) old friend; (O/Eng/Wel) fair-
haired.

Alec
(Greek) defender of humankind.
A form of Alexander.

Alem

(Arabic) wisdom.

Aleric
(German) ruler.

***Alex**
(Greek) defender of humankind.
A short form of Alexander/
Alexandra.

Alexander
(Greek) defender of humankind.

Alford
(Old English) wise advisor from
the old river crossing.

Alger
(Old German) noble spearman.

Algernon
(Old French) beard or moustache.

***Ali**
(Arabic) highly praised, great.

Allan
(Irish) harmony; peace; fair and
beautiful; bright and cheerful.
A masculine form of Alanna and
a form of Alan.

Almeric
(Old German) powerful ruler.

***Alon**
(Hebrew) oak; strength.

Alphonse
(Old German) noble and eager
to do battle.

***Alpin/*Alpine**
(Scottish) high mountains;
blond-haired.

Alric/Alrich
(Old German) hard and noble
ruler; fierce; wolf ruler; hard and
noble supreme ruler.

Alroy
(Old English) red-haired.

Alston
(Old English) noble town;
temple stone.

Amar
(Punjabi) immortal; (Arab) builder.

Ambrose
(Greek) immortal and divine.

***Amery**
(Old French) ruling worker.

Ames
(French) friend.

Amir
(Arabic) prince.

Ammon
(Egyptian) hidden; (Heb) son
of my people.

***Amory**
(Old German) famous and divine
ruler; (Lat) love.

Amos/Amoz
(Hebrew) burden; strength.

Amund
(Scandinavian) divine protector.

***An**
(Chinese/Vietnamese) peace.

***Ana**
(Tongan) cave.

Ancel
(Latin) servant.

Anders
(Greek/Swedish) strong and
courageous. A form of Andrew.

Andre
(Greek/Hebrew/French) strong and courageous. A form of Andrew.

Andrew
(Greek) strong and courageous.

*Angel/Angelo
(Greek) messenger of God; angel. A masculine form of

Angela/Angelina.
Angus
(Scottish) possessor of strength.

*Anh
(Vietnamese) safety; peace.

*Anlon
(Scottish) great champion.

*Annan
(Scottish) stream.

*Anoke
(Native American) one who acts out a story; actor.

Ansel
(Old French) under God's protection.

Anselm
(Old Norse/Old German) warrior with divine protection.

*Anslee/*Ansleigh/*Ansley
(Old English) meadow of inspiration.

Anson
(Hebrew/Old English) Anne's son; son of the graceful one.

Anthony
(Latin) priceless.

Anwar
(Arabic) ray of light.

Arad
(Hebrew) dragon.

Araldo
(Spanish/Scandinavian) ruler of the army. A form of Haraldo.

Aram
(Hebrew) highly praised; height.

Aran
(Thai) forest; (Heb) ark.

Archer
(Old English) bow user, archer.

Ardell
(Latin) eager.

*Arden
(Latin) glowing valley.

*Ardlee/*Ardleigh/*Ardley
(Latin/Old English) glowing meadow.

Argyle
(Scottish) from Ireland.

*Ari
(Hebrew) strong and worthy lion.

Aric
(Old English) ruler.

*Arion
(Greek) mythological magic horse.

Arkell
(Old Norse) eagle cauldron.

Arki/Arkie/Arkin
(Norwegian) son of the eternal king.

Arlo
(Greek/Latin) strong and courageous.

A form of Andrew.

*Arlyn
(Old English) hare pool.

Armand
(Greek/Old German) strong and
courageous army.

Armon
(Hebrew) castle.

*Arran
(Scottish) island.

Art/Artie/Arthur
(English) rock; (Ir) noble strength;
(Scot) bear. A short
form of names starting
with 'Art' e.g. Arthur.

Ascott
(Old English) cottage in
the east.

*Ash
(Hebrew) ash tree; (Eng)
ashes. A short form of Ashley.

*Ashburn
(Old English/Scottish) ash
tree stream.

*Ashford
(Old English) ash tree river
crossing.

*Ashley
(Old English) ash tree
meadow.

*Ashton
(Old English) ash tree
town.

*Ashwin
(Hindi) star; (Eng/Wel) fair
ash tree; ash tree friend.

Astley
(Greek/Old English) star-lit
meadow; (O/Eng) eastern
meadow.

Aston
(Old English) eastern town.

*Auden
(Old English) old valley.

*Audi/*Audie/*Audy
(German) noble strength.

*Audon
(Old English) old hill.

*Audun
(Scandinavian) deserted;
(O/Eng) old hill.

Auguste/Augustus
(Latin) majestic; royal one worthy
of honour; born in August. A
masculine form of Augusta.

Austin
(Latin) royal one worthy of
honour; born in August. A
masculine form of Augusta
and a form of Augustus.

Avel
(Russian) breath.

*Avery
(Old French) confirmation.

Avi
(Hebrew) my father.

*Awan
(Native American) important.

Axel/Axl
(Norse/Old German)
father of peace.

Aydin

(Turkish) intelligent.

B

Baden

(German) to bathe.

Badrick
(Old English) axe ruler.

Baelish
(Old French/Hebrew) Bailiff or
sheriff's officer; the man from
the bay.

Baez
(Welsh) boar.

Bahir
(Arabic) bright.

*Bailey
(Old French) bailiff or sheriff's
officer; one who pours water
from the meadow.

Bain
(Irish) fair-haired; (O/Eng) white
water. A short form of Bainbridge.

Bais
(Arabic) awake.

Bal
(Gypsy) hair; (Per) war advisor.

Balder
(Old English) bold army leader.

Balfour
(Scottish) village pastureland.

Balin
(Hindi) mighty warrior from the

stream.

Balint
(Hungarian) strength; (Lat) dancer;
(Lat) strength. A form of
Valentine.

Banan
(Irish) white.

Bancroft

(Middle English) bean field
in the secluded area.

Bane
(Hawaiian/Hebrew) son of the
farmer.

Banning
(Irish) little blond; (O/Eng) son
of the slayer.

*Bao
(Chinese) treasure.

Barack/Barak
(Hebrew) thunder.

Barclay
(Old English) clay meadow with
birch trees.

*Barden
(Old English) barley valley; the
poet's valley.

Bardrick
(German) axe ruler.

Barlow
(Old English) low barley meadow;
bare hill.

Barret
(German) strong like a bear.

Barris
(Old Welsh) son of Harris; son
of the army ruler.

Bart/Bartholomew
(Hebrew) son; son who suspends
the waters. A short form of
Bartholomew.

Barton
(Old English) barley town.

Bartram
(English) glorious raven.

Baxter
(Old English) baker.

Bear
(English) grizzly bear.

Beau
(Old French) handsome. A short
form of Beaumont.

Beaumont
(Old French) handsome
mountain.

*Bede
(Middle English) prayer.

Bejay
(French/English) handsome jay
bird.

Ben/Benny
(Hebrew) son of the right hand;
favourite. A short form of names
starting with 'Ben' e.g. Benjamin.

Benes
(Slavic) blessed.

Benito
(Italian/Latin) blessed.

Benjamin/Benji/
Benji
(Hebrew) son of the right hand;
favourite.

Benjiro
(Japanese) one who enjoys

peace.

Bennet
(Latin/French) little blessing.

Beno
(Mwera) member of the band;
(Heb) son.

Benoit
(French) blessed. A form of

Benedict.

Benson
(Hebrew) son of Benjamin; son
of the right hand; favourite son.

Bentlee/Bentleigh/
Bentley
(Old English) marsh meadow;
bent meadow.

Benton
(English) marsh town.

Benzi
(Hebrew) son of Zion; son
of the sign.

Berach
(Irish) marksman.

Berenger
(German) bear spearer.

Berg
(German) mountain.

Bergen
(French) shepherd; (Ger) hill.

Berger
(French) shepherd.

Bergren
(Scandinavian) mountain stream.

Bern
(German) bear.

*Berrigan
(Aboriginal) wattle.

Bevan
(English) son of Evan; well
born son; (Wel) glorious raven;
son of the warrior; (Celt) young
archer.

*Bevin
(Irish) sweetly singing.

Beynon
(Welsh) reliable.

*Billie/Billy
(German/Old English) wilful. A
short form of William.

*Birklee/*Birkleigh/
*Birkley
(Old English) birch tree meadow.

Bjorn
(Norse/Swedish) bear.

Blade
(Old English) prosperity and glory;
sword; grass (Ir) lean.

*Blain/*Blaine
(Old English) flame; (Ir) thin.

*Blair
(Irish) marsh plain; (Scot) field of
battle.

*Blaise
(English) burning flames; (Lat)
sprouting.

*Blake
(Old English) dark-haired;
dark-complexioned; black.

*Blakelee/*Blakeleigh/
*Blakeley
(Old English) black meadow.

*Blanco
(Spanish) white-haired.

Blandford
(Latin/Old English) mild river
crossing; blonde river crossing.

*Blasé/*Blaise/
*Blayse/*Blaze
(Greek) one who stammers.

Bly/Bligh
(Native American) high; (O/Eng)
happy. A short form of Blythe.

*Bo
(Chinese) precious; (Eng/Fren)
handsome; (O/Nors) homeowner.
A form of Beau.

*Bobbie/*Bobby
(Old German/Old English)
famous and brilliant. A short
form of Robert.

Boden
(Scandinavian) shelter; (O/Fren)
messenger.

Bogart
(Old French) strong bow; (Dan)
archer.

Bolton
(Old English) manor town.

*Bon
(Latin) good.

Bonar
(Old French) courteous, gentle and
kind.

Bonaro
(Italian/Spanish) good friend.

Bond
(English) one who tills the soil;
(Ice) soil stayer.

Bono
(Latin) good. A masculine form
of Bona.

Booker
(Old English) book reader; book
maker.

Boone
(Old French) good; blessing.

Borden
(Old English) valley of boars.

Borg
(Old Norse) settlement; (Scan)
castle.

Bosley
(Old English) boar meadow.

Boston
(Old English) boar town.

Boswell
(Old English) boar stream.

Bourn/Bourne
(Scottish) stream.

Boutros
(Arabic/Greek) rock. A form
of Peter.

Bowen
(Old English) son of Owen; son
of the well born one; (Ir) little
and victorious.

*Bowie
(Irish) blond-haired.

Boyd
(Scottish) fair-haired.

Boyne
(Irish) white cow; white river.

Bradburn
(Old English/Scottish) broad

stream.

Braden/Brayden
(Old English) broad valley;
(Ir) salmon.

Bradford
(Old English) broad river
crossing.

Bradley

(Old English) broad meadow;
(Scot) clearing in the woods.

Bradman
(Old English) broad man.

Bradon
(English) broad hill.

Bradshaw
(Old English) broad forest; broad
shore.

Bradwell
(Old English) broad stream.

Brady
(Irish) spirited; long island;
(Eng) broad.

*Brae
(Scottish) hill.

Braeden/Braiden/Braidon/
Braidyn/Brayden/Braydin/
Braydon/Braydyn
(Scottish/Old English) hill valley.

Bram
(Hebrew) high father. A form
of Abraham/Abram and a short
form of names starting with 'Bram'
e.g. Bramwell.

Bramwell
(Old English) bramble bush
stream.

Bran
(Irish) raven.

Branch
(Latin) paw; tree branch.

Brand
(Old English) torch or beacon. A
short form of names starting
with 'Brand' e.g. Brandon.

Brandan/Branden/Brandin/
Brandon/Brandyn
(Irish) youthful, bold and brave;
raven; (O/Eng) torch or beacon
in the valley.

Branden
(Old English) torch or beacon
in the valley.

Brander
(Old Norse) torch or beacon;
sword.

Brando
(Old English) raven.

Brandon
(Old English/Irish) raven.

Brandt
(English) proud raven; beacon.

Brannon
(Irish/Old English) torch or
beacon on the hill.

Branson
(Irish/Old English) son of
Brandon; son of the raven.

Brant
(Old English) torch.

Branwell
(Irish) raven from the stream.

Brawley
(Old English) hill meadow.

Braxton
(English) Brock's town; badger
town.

Bray
(Old English) brow or top of
the hill.

Breck/Breik
(Irish) freckled.

Brencis
(Latin) crowned with laurel;
victory.

Brendan
(Irish) little raven; (Ir) sword;
torch or beacon valley.

Brennan
(Irish) water; water deliverer.

Brent
(Old English) steep hill. A short
form of Brenton.

Brenton
(Old English) town on the
steep hill.

Brett
(Irish/Scottish) from Britain.

Brewster
(English) brewer of beer.

Brice/Bryce
(Scottish/Welsh) ambitious; (Celt)
son of Rhys; son of the ardent
and enthusiastic one.

Brick
(English) bridge; house builder; brick.

Brighton
(English) from Brighton in
England; sunny town.

Brinley
(English) beacon or torch in the

wood meadow.

Brock
(Old English) badger.

Brod
(English) broad area; ruler; (Scan)
brother. A short form of
Broderick.

Broder

(Scandinavian) brother.

Broderick
(Welsh) son of Roderick; son
the renowned ruler; (Scan) brother.

Brodie/Brody
(Scandinavian) brother;
(Scot) second born son;
(Ir) canal builder; (Wel) son of
Roderick; son of the renowned
ruler. A short form of Broderick.

Brodney
(Slavic) by the stream; (O/Eng) famous
clearing

Bromley
(Old English) cleared meadow.

*Bron/Bronn
(Old English/German/Dutch)
brown.

Brone
(Irish) sorrowful.

Bronson
(Old English) Brown's son;
son of the brown/reddish-
complexioned one.

*Brook/*Brooke
(Old English) stream. A masculine
form of Brooke.

*Brooklyn
(Old English) pool by the stream.

Brown
(Middle English) brown-
complexioned; brown-haired.

Bryant
(Irish) hill; (Celt) strong and
honourable. A form of Bryan.

Bryce/Bryse
(Scottish/Welsh) ambitious; (Ir)

son of Rhys; son of the ardent
and enthusiastic one.

Bryden/Brydon
(English) from Bryden in England;
hill in the valley.

*Bryn
(Welsh) hill; (Lat) boundary.

*Brynmor
(Welsh) large hill; (Eng) hill in the
marshland.

Bryson
(Welsh) Bryce's son; ambitious; (Ir)
son of Rhys; son of the ardent
and enthusiastic one.

Bu
(Vietnamese) leader.

Buck
(Old English) male deer; buck.
A short form of Buckley.

Buckley
(Old English) buck or deer
meadow.

Burleigh
(Old English) castle meadow.

Burnaby
(Old Norse) the warrior's
estate.

Burne/Burnes
(Scottish) stream.

Burnell
(Old French) little brown-
haired one.

Burnett
(Old English) castle estate;
(Eng) burnt nettle.

Burney
(Old English) stream island; castle

estate. A short form of
Burnett.

Burnes/Burns
(Scottish) stream.

Byford
(Old English) near the river
crossing.

Byram
(Aramaic) celebration.

Byrne
(Irish) field on the summit;
(Scot) stream.

C

Cable

(Old English) rope maker.

*Cadal
(Irish) warrior.

Caddoc
(Welsh) war-like; warrior.

*Cade
(Welsh) warrior. A short form
of Cadell.

*Cadell
(Welsh/Irish/English) battle
in the valley; warrior from
the valley.

Cadman
(Irish) warrior.

*Caelan
(Irish) powerful in battle.

Caffar
(Irish) protection for the head in
battle, helmet.

Cahil
(Turkish) young and naïve; (Arab)
good friend.

Cain
(Irish/Scottish) tribute; (Wel)
beautiful; (Jap) golden; (Haw)
eastern sky; (Heb) spear; possession.

Cainan
(Hebrew) possess; lament.

Cairn
(Welsh) landmark
piled with stones.

Caldwell
(Old English) old stream; cold
stream.

*Cale
(Hebrew) faithful.

Caleb
(Hebrew/Arabic) faithful; bold; crow;
basket; heart; victorious dog (loyal).

*Caley
(Irish/Old English) slender
meadow.

Callaghan
(Irish) conflicted.

*Callan
(Aboriginal) the sparrow hawk;
(Ger) talker; (O/Nrs) to cry.

*Callis
(Latin) goblet or cup, chalice.

Callum
(Scottish) follower of St Columba;
gentle; (Ir) dove.

Calvin
(Latin) bald.

*Cam
(Vietnamese) sweet citrus;
(Gyp) loved; (Scot) crooked
or bent nose. A short form
of Cameron.

*Camden
(Irish) winding and windy valley.

*Cameron
(Scottish) crooked or bent nose.

*Camilo
(French/Tongan) ceremonial
attendant; (Lat) freedom.

Campbell
(Scottish) crooked or bent mouth;

(Fren) beautiful and bright field.

Canute/Kanute
(Scandinavian) knot; (Lat) white-
haired; (O/Nrs) race.

Carden

(Old French) one who combs
out wool or fibres, a card.

Cardew
(Old Welsh) black foot.

Cardle
(Irish) brave.

*Carey/*Cary
(Greek) pure; (Wel) castle on the
rocky island.

Carl
(Old German) strong and courageous.
The German form of Charles.

Carleton
(Old English) Charles' town; strong
and courageous one's town. A
form of Charlton.

*Carlin
(Irish) little champion.

Carlo/Carlos
(Old English/Italian) strong and courageous.
A form of Charles.

Carlton
(Old English) from Carl's/Charles'
town; the strong and courageous town.

Carlyle
(Irish) strengthened castle; (Eng)
Carl's island; strong and
courageous island.

Carmichael
(Scottish) friend of St Michael;
(Ir) castle of St Michael.

Carmine
(Latin) song; crimson colour, red.

Carnell
(English) defender of the castle.

Carney
(Irish) victorious warrior.

Carr
(Scandinavian/Norse) marsh;
(Ir) castle.

Carrick
(Scottish) rocky cliff.

Carson
(Old English/Irish) Car's son;
son from the castle; (Scand/Nrs/Eng)
son of the marsh.

Carswell
(Old English) watercress stream;
cart maker's stream.

Carter
(Old English) cart maker or driver.

Carvel
(Manx) song; (Fren) wood carver's
village.

Carver
(English) one who carves wood,
sculptor.

*Cary/*Carey
(Welsh) castle on the rocky island;
(O/Eng) carer; loving.

*Casey
(Irish) brave.

Cashel
(Irish) castle wall.

Cashlin
(Irish) little castle pool.

Casper
(Persian) gemstone; (Per) guardian
of the treasure. A form of Casper.

*Cassidy/*Kassidy
(Irish) clever; curly haired.

Cato
(Latin) cautious wisdom.

Cavan
(Irish) handsome. A form of Kevin
and a short form of Cavanaugh.

Cavanaugh
(Irish) handsome.

Cavell
(Old French) little and active;
(O/Eng) cave valley.

Cawley
(Scottish/Old Norse) ancient;
(O/Eng) cow meadow.

Chan
(Sanskrit) bright.

*Chance/Chancey
(Middle English) good fortune.

Channing
(Old French) high church official;
(Lat) singer; (Eng) young wolf;
young and fierce.

Chapman
(Old English) trader.

Charles
(German/French) strong and
courageous. A masculine form
of Charlotte/Carla.

*Charley/*Charlie
(German/English) strong and
courageous meadow. A short form
of Charles/Charlton.

Charlton
(German/Old English) strong
and courageous town.

Charro
(Spanish) rider of horses.

*Chase
(French) hunter.

*Chaska
(Sioux) first born.

*Chayton
(Lakota) falcon.

*Chaz
(German/English) strong and
courageous. A form of Charles.

*Chen
(Chinese) great.

*Cheney
(Old French) oak grove forest.

Cheng
(Chinese) correct.

Chepe
(Spanish) God has added a child;
increasing; perfect.
A form of Joseph.

Chet
(English) from Rochester in
England; (O/Eng) cottage.
A short form of Chetwin.

Chetwin
(Old English) cottage with a

winding path; (O/Eng/Wel)
white cottage.

Chevalier/Chevy
(French) knight.

*Cheyne
(Scottish) oak hearted; strength;
God is gracious. A form of Shane.

*Chi
(Nigerian) guardian angel; (Chin)
young.

Chico
(Spanish) young.

Chiko
(Japanese) arrow; promise.

Chilton
(Old English) the children's spring town.

*Chris/*Cris
(Greek) Christ bearer. A short form
of Christopher or Christine.

*Christian/*Christen
(Greek/Latin) Christian; Christ bearer.

Christof
(Greek/Russian) Christ bearer;
Christian. A form of Christopher.

Christopher
(Greek) Christ bearer; Christian.

*Cian
(Irish) ancient.

*Clancy
(Scottish) belonging to the family;
(Ir) red-haired.

Clarence
(Latin) bright. A masculine form
of Claire.

Clark
(Old French) scholar.

Clarkson
(Old French) Clark's son; son of
the scholar.

Claude
(French) little and weak. A masculine
form of Claudette.

Claus
(German/Greek) victory of the
people. A form of Nicholas.

Clay
(Old English) earth.

Clayborn/Clayborne/
Claybourn/Claybourne

(Old English) born of earth,
(Eng/Scott) clay stream.

Clayton
(Old English) town built on clay.

Cleary
(Irish) scholar.

Cleveland
(Old English) cliff land.

Cliff
(Old English) cliff.

Clifford
(Old English) river crossing at the
side of the cliff.

Clifton
(Old English) town near the cliff.

Clint
(English) hill. A short form of Clinton.

Clive
(Old English) cliff.

Clyde
(Scottish) high and rocky area
of land; (Ir) heard from afar.

*Coby
(Hebrew) maintainer. A short
form of Jacob.

*Cody
(Old English) cushion;
(Ir/Scott) helpful.

*Colby
(English) coal town; dark-haired.

Cole
(Irish) promise; (M/Eng) coal.

Colson
(English) Col's son; son from the
coal town.

Colt

(English) young horse.

Colter
(English) herd of colts.

Colton
(English) black town; coal town.

Colwyn
(Welsh) hazel grove; (O/Eng) coal
friend.

Compton
(Old English) valley town.

Con/Conn
(Irish) desire; (Lat) steadfast. A
short form of Connor or
Constantine.

Connor
(Irish) desire.

Conroy
(Irish) wisdom; desired king;
persistent. A combination of
Con and Roy.

Conway
(Welsh) holy water; (Ir) hound
from the plains.

Cook
(English) chef.

Cooper
(Old English) barrel maker.

Corbett/Corbin
(Old French) raven; dark-haired.

*Corey/*Cori/*Cory
(Irish) hollow; (Ger) helmet.

Cormac
(Scottish) chariot racer; (Grk)
tree trunk.

Corrigan

(Irish) spear bearer.

Corrin
(Irish) spear carrier.

Cortez
(Spanish) courteous.

Corwin
(Scottish) beyond the hill;
(O/Eng/Wel) white heart.

Costa
(Greek) steadfast. A short form of
Constantine.

Creighton
(Scottish/English) town on
the rocks.

Creswell
(Old English) stream where the watercress
grows.

Culley
(Irish) woodland.

Curt/Curtis
(English) courtier, attendant at the court;
(O/Fren) courteous; (Lat) courtyard.

*Cynan
(Welsh) chief.

D

Daario
(Spanish) wealthy.

*Dacey
(Irish) southerner.

*Dai
(Japanese) great; (Eng) born
during the day.

*Dal
(Scandinavian) valley.

*Dalby
(Old English) village in the valley.

*Dale
(Old English) valley.

*Dallan
(Irish) unseeing.

*Dallas
(Scottish) waterfall valley.

*Dalman
(Aboriginal) place of plenty.

Dalston
(English) from Daegel's town;
from Daegel, England; town in
the valley.

Dalton
(Old English) valley town.

Dalziel
(Scottish) small field.

Damario
(Spanish) gentle.

Damon
(Greek) tamed; constant; (Lat)
spirit.

Dan
(Hebrew) God is my judge. A short
form of names starting with 'Dan'
e.g. Daniel.

Dancel
(Dutch) God is my judge.

Dandre
(French/Greek) strong and
courageous. A form of Andre/
Andrew.

Dane
(Danish) from Denmark.

Daniel
(Hebrew) God is my judge. A
masculine form of Danielle.

*Dannon
(Hebrew/Old English) God is my
judge; gathering in the meadow.

*Dany/*Danny
(Hebrew/English) God is my judge.
A short form of names starting with
'Dan' e.g. Daniel.

Dante
(Italian/Spanish) lasting. A form of
Durante.

*Danyon
(Hebrew/Old English) God is my
judge.

*Darby
(Irish) freedom.

*Darcy
(Old French) fortress.

*Darion
(Spanish) gift.

Darius
(Persian) ruler; (Grk) wealthy.

Darkon

119

(Old English) dark.

Darrie
(Irish) red-haired. A form of Derry.

David
(Hebrew) beloved.

*Davin
(Scandinavian) bright one from
Finland.

Davis
(Hebrew/English) son of David;
beloved son.

Davos
(Hebrew/English) son of David;
beloved son. A form of Davis.

Dawson
(Hebrew/English) David's son;
beloved son.

Dax
(French/English) water.

Dayan
(Hebrew) God is my judge. A form
of Daniel.

*Daylon
(African) American the day is long.

Dayne/Dane
(Scandinavian) from Denmark.

Dayton
(English) sunny town; day town.

De
(Chinese) virtuous.

Deacon
(Greek/English) dusty servant.

Dean
(Old English) valley; (Fren) leader.

*Deandre

(French/Greek) strong and
courageous gift. A combination of
Andre and David.

Deangelo
(Italian/Greek) angel, messenger
of God.

Decarlos
(Spanish/English) strong and
courageous. A form of Charles.

Declan
(Irish) praying; (Eng) the clan member.

Dejuan
(Spanish/Hebrew) God is gracious.
A form of John.

*Del
(French) of the (used as a prefix to
other names); (O/Eng) valley.

*Delaney
(French/Irish) elder tree grove;
(Eng) valley lane; (Ir) the
challenger's descendant.

Delano
(German) noble protector;
(Old French) night; (Lat) alder grove.
A masculine form of Delana.

Delfino
(Latin/French) from Delphi; dolphin.

*Dell
(English) small valley.

Dellinger
(Scandinavian) day spring.

*Delmar
(Latin/Old French) sea.

Delmon
(English/French) mountain.

*Delsin
(Native American) truthful.

*Delton
(English) valley town.

Delvin
(English) Godly friend.

Dempsey
(Irish) proud.

Dempster
(Old English) judge.

Denby
(Scandinavian) from the village
of Denby.

Denell
(Hebrew/African American)
God is my judge. A masculine
form of Danielle.

Denham
(Old English) valley village.

Denley
(Old English) meadow valley.

Denman
(Old English) man from the valley.

Dennison
(Greek/Old English) Dennis's son;
son of the follower of Dionysus,
the God of wine.

Denny
(Greek) follower of Dionysus, the
God of wine.

Denton
(English) valley town.

Denvor
(Old English) valley village.

Denzel
(Cornish) high; valley fortress.

Denzo
(Japanese) discretion.

Dequan
(Comanche) fragrant.

*Derain
(Aboriginal) mountains.

Deron
(Hebrew) bird.

*Derry
(Irish) red-haired; from Derry
in England.

Derryn
(Welsh) little bird.

Derwin
(Welsh) beloved friend; beloved
and fair-haired.

*Deven
(Hindi) for God; (Scot) beloved.

*Devin
(Irish) poet; people of the deep valley.

Devlin
(Irish) fierce and brave.

Dex/Dexter
(English) dyer of fabrics; (Lat)
skillful right hand.

*Dian
(Indonesian) candle.

Diego
(Hebrew/Spanish) maintainer. A
form of James.

Digby
(Old Norse) farm by the ditch.

Diggory
(Cornish) almost lost.

*Dillon
(French) lion-like; (Ir) faithful.

*Dimiter/Dimitri
(Greek) of Demeter, the Goddess
of fertility; lover of the earth.

Dino
(Italian/Spanish) valley. A form
of Dean.

*Dion
(Greek) of Dionysus, the God
of wine.

Dirk/Dierk/Dierks
(German) gifted ruler of the people.

Dixon
(English) rich, powerful and hard

ruler. A form of Richard.

Dolan
(Irish) dark and bold.

Dolby
(Old English) village in the valley.

Dominic
(Latin) belonging to God.

Donegal
(Irish) fort of foreigners.

Donnell
(Irish) dark-haired warrior.

Donovan
(Irish) dark-haired warrior.

Dooley
(Irish) dark-haired warrior.

Doran
(Irish) stranger; (Grk) gift.

Dorby
(Irish/Old English) village by the
stream.

Dore/Dor
(Irish) stream. (Hebrew)
generation.

Dougal
(Scottish/Irish/Gaelic) dark
stranger.

*Dover
(Hebrew) water; speaker.

*Drew
(Scottish) strong and courageous. A
short form of Andrew.

Drover
(English/Australian) sheep or
cattle herder.

Duff/Dugan
(Scottish) black-haired.

Duncan
(Old English) dark-haired warrior.

*Dusty
(English) covered in dust. A
short form of Dustin.

*Dylan
(Irish) sea.

E

12

Ean
(English/Scottish) God is gracious.
A form of Ian.

Earl
(Irish) promise; (Eng) noble.

Easton
(English) eastern town.

Eaton
(English) estate town by the river.

Eben
(Hebrew) rock.

*Edan
(Irish) fire.

Eddard
(Old English) wealthy guardian.
A short form of Edward.

Edel
(German) noble.

*Eden
(Hebrew) delightful; paradise.

*Edin
(Irish/Scottish) God is gracious. A
form of John.

Edison/Eddison
(Old English) Edward's son; son of the
wealthy friend.

Edward
(Old English) wealthy ruler.

Edwin
(English/Welsh) wealthy friend;
wealthy and fair-haired.

*Egan
(Irish) fiery.

Egon

(German) formidable.

*Eiddwen
(Welsh) fond and faithful.

*Einar
(Scandinavian) individual;
(Nrs) warrior chief.

*Eion
(Irish/English/Scottish) God
is gracious. A form of Ian.

Ekon
(Nigerian) strength.

Elam
(Hebrew) highlands.

Elan
(Native American) friend; (Heb)
tree.

Eldon
(English) elder tree hill.

Elek
(Greek/Hungarian) defender
of humankind. A form of Alec.

Eli
(Hebrew) uplifting; strong lord. A
short form of Elijah.

*Elian
(Hebrew) uplifting; strong lord; the
lord is my God. A form of Elijah.

Elias
(Greek/Hebrew) uplifting; strong lord;
the lord is my God. A form of Elijah.

Elijah
(Hebrew) uplifting; strong lord; the
lord is my God.

Elim
(Hebrew) ram.

Eljon

(Syrian) going up.

*Elk
(Native American) large deer.

*Ellery
(English) alder tree island.

*Ellis/*Ellison
(English/Hebrew) the lord is
my God; Ellis' son.

Ely
(Hebrew) uplifting; strong lord; the
lord is my God. A short form
of Elijah.

*Emerson
(German/Old English) Emery's
son, hardworking son.

*Emery
(German) hard working ruler.

Emil
(Gothic) hard working; (Lat)
flatterer.

Emile/Emilio
(German) hard working; (Lat)
eager to please.

Emmanuel
(Hebrew) God is with us.

Emmett
(German) hard working; strong;
(O/Eng) little ant.

Emory
(German) hard working ruler.

Enan
(Welsh) anvil, hammer.

Endor
(Hebrew) fountain; adorable. A
masculine form of Endora.

Endre

(Greek) strong and courageous. A
form of Andre.

Eric/Erik
(Scandinavian) wealthy ruler; (Ger)
ruler. A masculine form of

Erica/Erika.

*Erie
(Native American) place where
the panther resides.

Espen
(Danish) bear.

Essien
(Ochi) sixth born.

Este
(Italian) east.

Ethan
(Hebrew) strength.

*Etienne
(French/Greek) crowned. A
form of Stephen/Steven.

*Etu
(Native American) sunny.

Euan
(Scottish) young warrior.

Evan
(Welsh) son of Evan; well born son;
(Wel) glorious raven; son of the
warrior (Celt) young archer.

Evander
(Greek) preacher.

Everett/Rhett
(English) mighty; (Wel) ardent,
enthusiastic.

*Everlee/*Everleigh/
*Everley
(Old English) Evan's meadow;
well born one's meadow; God's

gracious meadow.

Everton
(English) mighty town; well born
town; God's gracious town.

*Evron/*Evvron
(Hebrew/Irish) fruitful.

Ewan
(Welsh) God is gracious.

Ewen
(Irish) noble friend; God is gracious.

Eyar
(Norse) island warrior.

*Eyota
(Native American) great.

Ezekiel
(Hebrew) strength of God.

Ezra
(Hebrew) helper.

F

*Fallon
(Irish/Scottish) the ruler's
grandchild.

*Fane
(English) happy; bull or
sheep meadow.

Farid
(Arabic) duty; unique.

Faris
(Arabic) horseman.

Farnell
(English) hill covered with ferns.

Faste
(Norwegian) firm.

*Faxon
(German) long-haired.

Fazio
(Italian) good worker.

Fedor
(Russian) gift of God. The Russian
form of Theodore.

Felipe
(Spanish) lover of horses.

Felix
(Latin) fortunate.

Fenton
(Old English) marsh town; enclosure
town.

Feodor/Feodore
(Slavic/Greek) gift of God. A

form of Theodore.

Fergus
(Irish) strength; (Celt) choice;
(Ger/Goth) life adventure. A

form of Ferdinand.

Fernando
(Spanish/German) adventurous.

Ferran
(Arabic) baker.

Ferrell
(Irish) hero.

Ferris
(Scottish) rock; (Ir) choice. A
form of Peter.

Fidel
(Latin) faithful.

Fife
(Scottish) from Fife in Scotland.

Finbar
(Irish) fair-haired chief.

*Findlay
(Irish/Scottish) fair-haired
warrior.

Fineas
(Irish/Hebrew) oracle; (Egypt)
dark-complexioned.

Finian
(Irish) fair-haired child.

*Finlay
(Irish) blonde-haired.

Finn
(Irish/Scottish) fair-haired;
fair-complexioned; (O/Ger)
from Finland.

Finnegan
(Irish) fair complexioned.

Fintan
(Irish) Finland; Finn's town.

Fiorello/Fiorelli
(Latin) little flower.

Firas
(Arabic) persistent.

Fiske
(English) fish.

Fitch
(English) weasel.

Fitz
(Old English) son. A short form
of names beginning with 'Fitz' e.g.
Fitzgerald.

Fitzgerald
(Old English) son of Gerald; son
of the brave spear carrier.

Fitzpatrick
(Old English) Patrick's son; noble
son.

Fitzroy
(French) son of Roy, the king's
son.

Flann
(Irish) red-haired.

Fleming
(Old English) lowlands; (Dutch)
one.

Fletcher
(Old French) arrow maker.

Flint
(Old English) rock; brook.

Floranz
(Latin) flowering.

*Florent
(French) flowering.

*Flynn
(Irish/Scottish) son of the
red-haired one; son of Finn.

*Fontaine

(French) fountain.

Forbes
(Irish/Scottish) wealthy field;
(Scot) headstrong.

Ford
(Old English) river crossing.

Fordel
(Gypsy) forgiven.

Fordon
(German) destroyer.

Foster
(Old English) guardian of
the forest.

Fox
(Old English) fox.

Franklin
(Old English) honest stream;
freedom stream.

Fraser
(Old French) strawberry; (O/Eng)
curly-haired.

Frederick
(German) king of peace.

Freeman
(Old French) free man.

Fremont
(German) guardian of freedom.

*Frey
(English) the lord; (Nrs) fertility,
prosperity and peace. A masculine

form of Freya.

Fritz
(German) peaceful ruler.

Fyfe
(Scottish) from Scotland.

*Fynn
(Ghanaian) river; (Ir/Scott)
fair-haired; fair-complexioned;
(O/Ger) from Finland.

G

*Gabe
(Hebrew) strength of God. A short
form of Gabriel.

*Gabriel
(Hebrew) strength of God. A short
form of Gabriel and a masculine
form of Gabrielle.

Gage
(French) promise.

Gair
(Irish) small.

Galbraith
(Irish) Scottish person living in
Ireland.

*Galen
(Old English) lively and merry;
harsh wind; (Heb) born of a
joyous father. A masculine form
of Gail/Abigail.

Galeran
(French) healthy ruler.

Gallagher
(Irish) eager helper.

Galloway
(Irish) by the gallows; (Ir) Scottish
person living in Ireland.

Galt
(Norwegian) high ground.

Galton
(English) rented land in

the town; (Nor/O/Eng) town
on the high ground.

Galvin
(Irish) bright; sparrow.

Gamlyn

(Old Norse) little and old.

Ganan
(Aboriginal) west.

Gannon
(Irish) light complexioned.

Garcia
(Spanish/German) brave hard
spear. A form of Gerald.

Garek
(Polish/English) successful spearer.
A form of Edgar.

Gareth
(Welsh) gentle and old.

*Gariana
(Hindi) to yell.

Garman
(Welsh) from Germany.

*Garner
(English) gatherer; (Fren) army
guardian.

*Garnet
(Middle English) dark red
precious gem.

Garnock
(Welsh) alder tree river.

Garrad
(English/Irish) brave spearer.

Garrett
(Old English/German) hard
spearer; brave spearer. A form
of Gerald.

Garrick
(German) mighty spear ruler.

Garrie
(Aboriginal) emu; sleepy.

Garrin

(English/German) mighty
spearer.

Garrison
(Old English) Gary's son;
spearer's son; (Fren) troops
stationed at the fort.

Garth
(Scandinavian) spearer's
enclosure.

Garton
(English) triangular-shaped
town.

Garve
(Scottish) rough place.

Garvey
(Irish) peace.

Garvin
(German) friend who is
in strife.

Garwood/Gurwood
(English) forest with the
fur trees.

Gaspar
(Spanish/Persian) guardian
of the treasure. A form
of Casper.

Gaston
(French) from Gascony, France.

Gatier
(French/German) ruling
people; powerful warrior.
A form of Walter.

Gavrie
(Russian) belonging to God.

Gavriel
(Hebrew) strength of God. A
form of Gabriel and a masculine

form of Gabrielle.

Gawain
(Welsh) hawk. A form of Gavin.

Gawath
(Welsh) hawk of battle.

Geary
(Middle English) changes.

Gendry
(English) gentle and kind.

Geno
(Italian) noble; well born.

Gentry
(English) gentle and kind.

George
(Greek) farmer.

Geraint
(Welsh) old.

Gerlach
(Scandinavian) spearer.

Germain
(French) from Germany.

Gervase
(German) honourable.

Gerwyn
(Welsh) fair love.

Geshem
(Hebrew) raining.

*Gi
(Korean) brave.

Giacinto
(Portuguese/Spanish) hyacinth;
purple. A form of Jacinto.

Giacomo
(Hebrew/Italian) maintainer. A

form of Jacob.

Giancarlo
(Hebrew/Italian) God is gracious,
strong and courageous. A
combination of Gian and Carlos,
John and Charles.

Gibson
(Old English) Gilbert's son;
trusted son.

Gil
(Greek) shield carrier; (Heb) happy.
A short form of names starting
with 'Gil' e.g. Gilbert.

Gilby
(Scandinavian) estate of the
hostage; (Ir) blonde-haired.

Gildea
(Irish) God's servant.

Gilen
(German/Basque) illustrious
promise.

Giles
(Greek) carrier of the shield.

Gilmore
(Irish) devoted marshland.

Gilon
(Hebrew) circle.

Gilroy
(Irish) devoted to the king.

Gilus
(Scandinavian) shield.

Gino
(Italian) noble; well born.

Giosia
(Hebrew/Italian) saviour. A
form of Joshua.

Giovanni
(Hebrew/Italian) God is gracious.
A form of John.

Gitano
(Spanish) gypsy.

Giulio
(Latin/Italian) youthful. A
form of Jules.

Giustino
(Latin/Italian) just. A
form of Justin.

Gjosta
(Swedish) God's staff.

Gladstone
(English) boundary stone;
happy estate.

***Glen/*Glenn/*Glyn/
*Glynn**
(Scottish) valley.

*Glendon
(Scottish) valley fortress.

Glenton
(Scottish/Old English) valley town.

Glenworth
(Scottish/Old English) valley farm.

***Glyn/*Glynn/*Glen/
*Glenn**
(Scottish/Welsh) small valley. A
form of Glen/Glenn.

Gough
(Welsh) red-haired.

Grady
(Irish) noble and illustrious.

Granger
(Old English) farmer.

Grant
(French) great.

Grantley
(French/Old English) great
meadow.

Gray/Grey
(Old English) grey colour.

Grayson/Greyson
(Old English) grey son.

Greeley
(Old English) grey meadow.

Gregor
(Greek) watchful.

Gregory
(Greek) watchful.

Griffin
(Latin) hooked nose.

Gunnar
(German/Scandinavian) bold.

Gunther
(German) battle army.

Gus
(Scandinavian) staff. A short
form of Gustav.

Gustav
(Swedish) noble staff bearer.

Guthre
(Irish) windy.

Guy
(French) guide from the forest;
(Eng) man.

Gwern
(Welsh) alder tree.

Gwylym
(German) Wilful. A form
of William.

H

Haakan
(Scandinavian) chosen son.

Haddad
(Arabic) blacksmith.

Haddon
(Old English) heather covered
hill.

Hadi
(Arabic) guidance to the right.

*Hadley
(Old English) heather meadow.

Hagan
(Irish) ruler of the home. A
form of Henry.

Hagar
(Hebrew) forsaken.

Hagen
(Irish/Scottish) little or
young.

Hai
(Vietnamese) sea.

Haines
(Old English) fence.

Hakan
(Native American) fiery.

Hakon
(Scandinavian) praised; (O/Nrs)
useful.

Hal
(Old English) hall. A short

form of names starting
with 'Hal' e.g. Halford.

Halbert

(Old English) brilliant; hero.

Haldane
(Scandinavian) half Danish.

Hale
(Old English) hero; hall.

*Halen
(Swedish) hall.

*Haley
(Irish/Scottish) ingenious;
(O/Eng) meadow hall.

Halford
(Old English) hall by the shallow
river crossing.

*Halian
(Zuni) youthful.

Halifax
(Old English) holy field.

Halil
(Turkish) close friend.

Halim
(Arabic) gentle.

Hallam
(Old Norse) rock; (O/Eng)
sloping valley.

*Hallan
(English) hall; manor.

Halton
(English) town on the hill.

Halvor
(Norwegian) rock; protector.

Halyard
(Scandinavian) rock defender.

Hamal
(Arabic) lamb; a star in the Aries
constellation.

Hamid
(Arabic) thanking God.

Hamill
(English) proud mill.

Hamilton
(Old English) proud town;
crooked hill.

Hamish
(Scottish) remover.

Hamlet
(Old French) little home.

Hamlin
(Old French/German) little
home lover; (Eng) village pool.

Hammet
(English/Scandinavian) village.

Hammond
(English) village.

Hamon
(German) home.

Hampton
(English) proud town.

Hanan
(Hebrew) graceful.

Handel
(German/English) God is
gracious. A form of John.

*Handley
(English) clearing in the forest.

Hanford
(Old English) high river
crossing.

Hank
(American/German) chief.

*Hanley
(Old English) high meadow.

Hannes
(Finnish) God is gracious. A
form of John.

Hanno
(German/Hebrew) God is
gracious. A form of John/
Johann.

Hans
(Scandinavian/Hebrew) God is
gracious. A form of John.

Hansel
(Scandinavian) God is gracious. A
form of John/Johann.

Hanson
(Scandinavian) son of Hans;
gracious son.

Hao
(Chinese) good.

Haral
(Scottish) army leader.

Harald
(Scandinavian/English) army
ruler. A form of Harold.

Harel
(Hebrew) God's mountain.

Harish
(Hindi) lord.

Harkin
(Irish) dark red-colour; red-haired.

Harlan/Harland
(Old English) hare land; rocky land;
battle land.

*Harley
(Old English) hare meadow.

*Harlow
(Old English) low hill of the
hare; battle hill.

Harmen/Harmens
(Dutch) harmonious. A masculine

form of Harmony.

Harmon
(German) man of the army.

Harold
(Old Norse) army ruler.

*Harper
(Old English) player of harps.

Harrington
(Old English) Harry's town;
the army ruler's town.

Harris
(Old English/Scandinavian)
Harry's son; the army
ruler's son.

Harrison
(Old English/ Scandinavian)
Harry's son; the
army ruler's son.

Harrod
(Hebrew) conquering hero.

Harry
(Old English/Scandinavian)
army ruler. A short form of names
starting with 'Harr' e.g. Harold.

*Hartley/*Hartly
(Old English) deer meadow.

Harvey
(German) army warrior;
(Celt) eager for battle.

Harwood
(English) the hare's forest.

Hasad
(Turkish) harvesting.

Hasant
(Swahili) handsome.

Hashim
(Arabic) destroyer of evil.

Hasim
(Arabic) determined.

Hasin
(Sanskrit) laughing one.

Haskel
(Hebrew) understanding.

Haslett
(Old English) little hazel tree.

Hassan
(Arabic) handsome.

Hassel
(English) the witch's corner;
from Hassall, England.

*Hassun
(Algonquin) stone.

*Hatiya
(Native American) bear.

Hau
(Vietnamese) desired.

*Haven
(English) refuge.

Havgan
(Irish) white.

Hawk/Hawke
(Old English/Saxon) One who
uses hawk game birds for hunting;
a hawk, a gaming bird.

Hawley
(English) hedged meadow.

Hawthorne
(English) hawthorn tree.

Hayden
(Old English) valley hedge.

Hayes
(Old English/Irish) place with
hedges.

Hayward
(Old English) guardian of the
hedged valley; guardian
of the hay.

Haywood
(Old English) forest hedge.

Heath
(Old English) heather. A short form
of names starting with
'Heath' e.g. Heathcote.

Heathcliff
(Old English) heather on
the cliff.

Heathcote
(Old English) cottage in the
heather.

Hedley
(Old English) meadow hedge;
sheep meadow.

Heinrich
(German) ruler of the house. A
form of Henry.

Hemene
(Nez Perce) wolf.

Henderick
(German/Dutch) ruler of the house.
A form of Henry.

Henderson
(Scottish/English) Henry's son; son
of the ruler of the house.

Hendrix
(German/Dutch) ruler of the house.
A form of Henry.

*Henley
(English) high meadow;
hen meadow.

Henry
(German) ruler of the house.

Herald
(English) news bringer; army
ruler.

Hernando
(German/Gothic/Spanish) life
adventure. A form of Ferdinand.

Herod
(Greek) protector.

Herrick
(German) army ruler.

Hew
(Welsh/German) intelligent;
(O/Ger) heart and mind.
A form of Hugh.

Hewett
(German) little Hugh; little
intelligent one.

Hewney
(Irish) green.

Hewson
(Welsh/German/English)
Hugh's son; son of the
intelligent one.

Heywood
(Old English) high woods.

*Hien
(Vietnamese) sweet.

*Hieu

(Vietnamese) respectful.

Hilal
(Arabic) new moon.

Hiroshi
(Japanese) generous; from
Hiroshima.

Hirsh
(Hebrew) deer.

Hiu
(Hawaiian) intelligent; (O/Ger)
heart and mind. A form of Hugh.

Hoa
(Vietnamese) peace loving.

Hoang
(Vietnamese) finish.

Hodor
(German/Old Norse/Old English)

door keeper (hold the door).

Hogan
(Irish/Scottish) youthful.

Holden
(Old English) hollow in the
deep valley.

Hollice/Hollis/Hollys
(Old English) holly tree grove.

Holt
(Old English) forest.

Horton
(Old English) grey town;
(Lat) garden.

Houghton
(Old English) grey town on a steep bank.

Houston
(Old English) hill town; Hugh's
town; the intelligent one's town.

Howard
(Old English) high guardian.

Howarth
(Old English) high farm;
(Anglo-Saxon) settlement on a hill.

Howell
(Welsh) little and alert.

Howi
(Moquelumnan) dove.

Howie
(English) high guardian. A short
form of Howard.

Howin
(Chinese) swallow of loyalty.

Howland
(Old English) high land; hill.

Hsu
(Chinese) promise; composed.

Hsuang
(Chinese) yellow; supreme.

*Hu
(Chinese) tiger.

*Hua
(Chinese) flower.

Hudson
(Old English) hooded son.

Huey
(Old English) intelligent;
(O/Ger) heart and mind.

Hugh/Hugo
(Old English) intelligent;
(O/Ger) heart and mind.

Hume
(Old Norse) river island;
(Ger) home lover.

*Hunter
(Old English) one who hunts.

*Huntley
(Old English) the hunter's meadow.

*Hurley
(Old English) clearing in the woods;
hare meadow; (Ir/Gae) sea tide.

*Hute
(Native American) star.

Hutton
(Old English) house in the town
over hanging a ledge.

Huxford
(Old English) Hugh's river crossing;
the intelligent one's river crossing.

*Huxley
(Old English) Hugh's
meadow; the intelligent
one's meadow.

Huy
(Vietnamese) glory.

Huyu
(Japanese) writer.

*Hy
(Vietnamese) hope.

*Hyatt
(Old English) high gate.

Hyde/Hyder
(Old English) measure of land,
acreage; tanner.

I

Iago
(Hebrew/Spanish) maintainer.
The Spanish form of James.

*Iakona
(Hawaiian) healer.

Ibrahim
(Hebrew/Arabic) high father.
The Arabic form of Abraham.

Ichiro
(Japanese) first born son.

*Idaho
(Native American) morning;
morning gem.

*Iden
(Old English) pasture in the
forest.

Ignatius
(Latin/Greek) fiery.

Imri
(Hebrew) tall.

Inar
(English) an individual.

Ince
(Hungarian) innocent.

Incencio
(Spanish) white; innocent.

*Ing
(Old Norse) famous.

Inger
(Old Norse) the son's army.

*Inglis/*English
(Scottish) English.

Ingmar
(Old Norse) Ing's son;
son of the famous one.

Ingram
(Old Norse) raven; angel.

*Inia
(Fijian) born under
a waterfall.

Inir
(Welsh) honourable.

*Innes
(Irish) island.

Iolo
(Welsh) worthy lord.

*Iona
(Hawaiian) dove; (Ir) island.

*Ira
(Aboriginal) camp; (Heb) watchful;
(Arab) stallion.

Iram
(English) bright.

Irfan
(Turkish) knowledgeable.

Irvin
(Scottish) green river.

*Isa
(Sanskrit) lord.

Isaac
(Hebrew) laughter; God smiles.

Isaiah
(Hebrew) God is generous;

God is my helper.

*Isi

(Choctaw) bear; (Heb) God smiles.
A short form of names starting
with 'Isi' e.g. Isidore or Isadora.

Isidore
(Greek) gift of Isis; (Eng) adored.
A masculine form of Isadora.

Issa
(Swahili) protected.

*Iva
(Russian) willow; (O/Fren)
yew tree; (Heb) God is gracious.

Ivan
(Hebrew) God is gracious. A
form of John.

Ivanhoe
(Hebrew) God's gracious tiller of
the soil.

Ivar
(Danish/Scandinavian) archer with
a yew bow.

Iven
(Old French) little yew bow.

Ives
(Old English) archer with a yew
bow.

Ivo
(Old French) yew tree; (O/Ger)
bow bearer.

Ivor
(Scandinavian) God.

*Iye
(Native American) smoke.

J

Ja
(Korean) attracting.

Jaan
(Estonian/Greek) Christian.

Jabari
(Swahili) fearless.

Jabbar
(Arabic) repairer.

Jabin
(Hebrew) understanding; to build.

Jabir
(Arabic) comforting.

Jacan
(Hebrew) trouble.

*Jace/Jas
(Greek/Australian) healer. A
short form of Jason.

Jacinto
(Spanish/Greek) beautiful;
(Heb) maintainer; (Span/Grk)
hyacinth; purple. A masculine
of Jacinta.

Jack
(Hebrew) maintainer.

Jackson
(Hebrew/Old English) Jack's son;
son of the maintainer.

Jacob
(Hebrew) maintainer. A form of
James.

Jacques
(Hebrew/French) maintainer.
The French form of Jack.

Jacy
(South American) moon;
(Greek) beautiful; (Span/Grk) purple;
hyacinth. A short form of Jacinto.

Jadon
(Hebrew) God has heard; repairer
of walls.

Jae Hwa
(Korean) prosperous.

Jaegar
(German) hunter.

Jafar
(Sanskrit) small stream.

Jagger
(English) driver of horses.

Jago
(Aboriginal) complete; (Span/Port)
maintainer. A form of James.

Jah
(Hebrew) everlasting.

*Jai
(Hebrew) God has enlightened;
illuminated; river. A short form
of Jairus.

*Jaiden
(Hebrew) God has heard.

Jake
(Hebrew) maintainer. A form
of James.

*Jal
(Gypsy) wanderer.

Jala
(Arabic) clarity.

Jalal/Jaleel
(Arabic) great.

*Jalen
(African American) calm.

Jalil
(Hindi) God-like.

Jalon
(Hebrew) murmur.

Jamar/*Jamara
(Arabic) handsome. A form
of Jamal.

Jamario
(Italian/French/American) warrior;
shining; war-like; dedicated to the
Virgin Mary. A form of Mario.

James
(Hebrew) maintainer.

Jameson/Jamison
(Hebrew/Old English) James' son;
son of the maintainer.

*Jamie/*Jaime/*Jamey
(Hebrew) maintainer. A
short form of James.

Jamil
(Arabic) handsome.

Jamin
(Hebrew) right hand; southern
wind.

Janek
(Hebrew/Polish) God is gracious.
A form of John.

Janoah
(Hebrew) resting.

Janos
(Hebrew/Hungarian) God is
gracious. A form of John.

Jansen
(Scandinavian) John's son; God's
gracious son.

Jaqen
(Hebrew/French) maintainer. A
form of Jacques.

Jaquan
(Comanche) scented. A form of
Quanah.

*Jarah/Jarrah
(Hebrew) sweet like honey;
red wood.

Jareb
(Hebrew) maintainer.

Jared
(Hebrew) ruling; (Grk) rose.

Jarek
(Slavic) born in January.

Jarell
(Scandinavian/German) brave
spearer. A form of Gerald.

Jareth
(Hebrew/Welsh) gentle
descendant.

Jarib
(Hebrew) avenger.

Jarl
(Norse) noble.

Jarman
(German) from Germany.
A form of Jermaine.

Jaron
(Hebrew) to cry or sing out.

*Jarrah
(Aboriginal) mahogany gum tree;
red wood.

Jarratt
(German) strong spearer.

Jarrell
(English/German) mighty spearer.
A form of Gerald.

Jarrett
(English/Hebrew) ruling.

Jarrod
(Hebrew) ruling.

Jas
(Hebrew/Polish/Australian) God
is gracious. A form of John and the
short form of names starting with
'Jas' e.g. Jason.

Jase
(Greek) healer. A short form
of Jason.

Jason
(Greek) healer.

Jasper
(Persian) gemstone; (Per) guardian of
the treasure. A form of Casper.

Jassan
(Native American) wolf.

Javan
(Hebrew) clay.

Javaris
(German) skilled spearer.

Javas
(Sanskrit) quick.

Javier
(Arabic) bright.

Javon
(Hebrew/American) God has
added a child; increasing; perfect. A
form of Joseph.

*Jay
(Latin/Old French) the jay bird.

Jaydon
(Hebrew) God has heard.

*Jaylee/*Jayley
(English) jay bird meadow.

Jaziel
(Hebrew) strength of God.

Jaziz
(Hebrew) brightness.

*Jazz
(English/American) lover or player
of Jazz music.

Jedrek
(Polish) strength.

Jefferson
(German/French/Old English)
son of Jeffrey; son of God's peace.

Jefford
(English) God's peaceful river
crossing.

Jehan
(Hebrew/French) God is gracious.
A form of John.

Jenkin
(Flemish) little John' God's gracious
little one.

Jeno
(Greek/Hungarian) noble and

wellborn; God is gracious. A form
of Eugene and a masculine form
of Eugenie.

Jens
(Scandinavian) God is gracious.
The Dutch form of John.

Jensen
(Dutch) God's gracious son. A form
of John.

Jered
(Hebrew) ruling.

Jeremiah
(Hebrew) praised highly by
God.

*Jericho
(Arabic) moon city.

Jeriel
(Hebrew) vision of God.

Jermaine
(French/German) from
Germany.

Jerod
(Hebrew) ruling.

Jeron
(English/Latin) holy.

Jerrick
(German) mighty spear ruler of
the people.

Jervis
(German) skilled spearer.

*Jesse/*Jessie/*Jessy
(Hebrew) wealthy. A short form
of Jesse. A masculine form of
Jessie or Jessica.

Jestin
(Welsh/Latin) just. A form of
Justin.

Jesus
(Hebrew) saviour.

Jethro
(Hebrew) excellence.

*Jett/*Jet
(Greek) black gemstone; (Eng)
black; gem; high speed plane.

*Jevan
(Welsh) noble and wellborn;
warrior; God is gracious. A form
of Evan.

Ji
(Chinese) order.

Jiao Long
(Chinese) dragon.

Jie
(Chinese) wonderful.

Jimeoin
(Irish/Hebrew/Australian)
noble maintainer. A combination
of Jim/Owen.

Jimmy/Jimi
(Hebrew) maintainer. A short form
of James.

Jing Quo
(Chinese) ruler.

Jiovanni
(Hebrew/Italian) God is gracious.
A form of John.

Jiro
(Japanese) second born.

Joah
(Hebrew) his brother is God.

*Joaquan/Joaquin
(Comanche) scented. A form of
Quanah.

*Joby
(Hebrew) sorrow. A form of

Job.

Jodan
(Hebrew) God is my judge.

Joe/Joey
(Hebrew) God has added a
child; increasing; perfect. A short
form of Joseph.

Joel
(Hebrew) God is willing.

Joergen
(Scandinavian) farmer. A form of
George.

Joffrey
(German/French) God's peace.

Johan/Johann
(German) God is gracious. A
form of John.

Johar
(Hindi) jewel.

John
(Hebrew) God is gracious.

Johnny
(Hebrew/English) God is gracious.
A form of John.

Jojen
(Hebrew/Welsh) God has added a
child; increasing white wave; perfect
white wave. A combination of Joe
and Jennifer.

*Jolon
(Native American) valley of dead
oak trees.

Jon
(Hebrew) God is gracious. A short
form of Jonathon/John.

Jonah
(Hebrew) dove; peace.

Jonas
(Hebrew) accomplished; God
is gracious. The Lithuanian form
of John.

Jonathon
(Hebrew) gift of God.

Jones
(Welsh) John's son; God's gracious
son.

*Jonty
(Hebrew/American) gift from
God.

*Jorah
(Hebrew) highly praised teacher.

*Joraj
(Hebrew) teacher.

Joram
(Hebrew) highly praised.

*Jordan/*Jorden/*Jordon
(Hebrew) river of judgement; descending.

Jorg
(German/Greek) farmer. A form
of George.

Jorin
(Hebrew/Sanskrit) child of freedom.

Joseph/Jose
(Hebrew) God has added a child;

increasing; perfect.

Josha
(Hindi) satisfied.

Joshi
(Swahili) to gallop.

Joshua
(Hebrew) God is my salvation.

(Dutch) God will uplift.

Josiah
(Hebrew) God will heal and
protect.

Joss
(Chinese) fate.

Jotham
(Hebrew) God is perfect.

Joubert
(Old English) shining.

*Jovan
(Latin) love; majestic; God is
gracious. A Slavic form of John.

*Jovi
(Latin) joy.

Juan
(Spanish) God is gracious. A form
of John.

*Jude
(Hebrew) confession; praise.

*Jules
(Latin/French/Greek) youthful.

*Julian/Julio
(Latin) youthful.

Julius
(Greek) youthful.

Jurgen
(German) farmer. A form of
George.

Juri
(Latvian) farmer.

Juro
(Japanese) best wishes for a
long life.

Jurrien

*Justice
(Old French) just.

Justin
(Old French) just.

K

Kabil
(Turkish/Hebrew) spear gatherer.

Kabir
(Arabic) great; history.

*Kacey
(Irish) brave.

Kadar
(Arabic) powerful.

*Kade
(Scottish) wetlands.

Kadeem
(Arabic) servant.

Kadin
(Arabic) friend.

Kadir
(Arabic) spring.

Kado
(Japanese) gateway.

*Kaelan
(Scottish) powerful warrior.

Kahil
(Turkish) young and naïve; friend.

*Kai
(Navajo) willow tree; (Haw) sea;
(Jap) to forgive; (Wel) keeper
of the keys.

*Kailen
(Irish) mighty warrior.

*Kain
(Hawaiian) spear thrower.

*Kaine
(Welsh) beautiful; (Ir) tribute;
(Haw) eastern sky.

*Kaj
(Danish) earth.

Kalat
(Arabic) castle.

Kaleb
(Hebrew/Arabic) faithful;
bold; crow; basket; heart;
victorious dog.

*Kalechi
(Nigerian) praise to God.

*Kalen
(Arabic) naïve.

*Kaleo
(Hawaiian) voice.

Kalevi
(Finnish) hero.

Kalid
(Arabic) eternal.

Kalil
(Arabic) good friend; (Turk)
young and naïve.

*Kalle
(English/Scandinavian) strong
and courageous.

*Kallen
(Irish) mighty warrior.

*Kalmin
(Scandinavian) man.

Kamal
(Hindi) lotus; (Arab) perfection.

Kamilo
(Tongan/French) ceremonial attendant; (Lat) freedom. A form of Camilo.

*Kana
(Japanese) powerful.

*Kanai
(Hawaiian) winner.

*Kanale
(Hawaiian) stony meadow.

*Kanaloa
(Hawaiian) God.

*Kane
(Irish/Scottish) tribute; (Wel) beautiful; (Jap) golden; (Haw) eastern sky; (Heb) spear possession. A form of Cain.

*Kangan
(Aboriginal) to cut.

*Kange/*Kangi
(Lakota) raven.

Kaniel
(Hebrew) stalk.

*Kanji
(Japanese) tin.

*Kanya
(Wemba-Wemba) breath; rock.

*Kaori
(Japanese) strength.

Karam
(Arabic) charitable.

Kardal
(Arabic) mustard seed.

Kare
(Norwegian) enormous.

Kareem
(Arabic) noble.

*Karem
(Wemba-Wemba) shield.

*Karey
(Greek) pure; (Wel) castle on the rocky island.

Karif
(Arabic) born in autumn.

Karl
(English) strong and courageous.

*Karney
(Irish) winning.

*Karr
(Scandinavian) marsh.

*Karsten
(Greek) anointment.

*Kasa
(Native American) robe made of fur.

Kaseem
(Arabic) divided.

Kasem
(Thai) happy.

Kasen
(Basque) helmet.

*Kasey
(Irish) brave.

Kasim
(Arabic) divided.

Kasper
(Persian) gemstone; (Per) guardian of the treasure. A form of Casper.

*Kassidy
(Irish) clever, curly haired.

Katen
(Wemba-Wemba) water.

*Kato
(Runyankore) second twin;
lake.

Kavan
(Irish) handsome. A form of
Kevin.

Kavanagh
(Irish) Kevin's follower;

handsome follower.

*Kawa
(Wemba-Wemba) mountain.

*Kayin
(Nigerian) celebrated; (Yor)
long hoped-for child.

*Keal
(Old Norse) ridge.

Keane
(Old English) eager; sharp.

Keanu
(Hawaiian) sea breeze.

Kearn
(Irish) dark.

Keaton
(English) where hawks fly.

Kedar
(Hebrew) dark; (Arab) powerful;
(Hind) mountain lord.

Keddy
(English) red earth; man. A form
of Adam.

Kedem
(Hebrew) ancient.

Kedrick
(Welsh) gift; (O/Eng) war
chief. A form of Cedric.

*Kee Lin
(Chinese) little dragon.

Keegan
(Irish/Scottish) small and fiery.

*Keelan
(Irish/Scottish) slender;
islander.

*Keeley
(Irish) handsome.

Keenan
(Irish/Scottish) little ancient
one.

Keene
(German) bold and sharp.

Kees
(Dutch/Greek) cornel tree; (Lat)
horn-coloured.

Keiffer
(German) cooper, barrel maker.

*Keiji
(Japanese) cautious ruler.

*Keir
(Scottish) dark in colour. A short
form of Keiren/Kieran.

Keitaro
(Japanese) blessed.

*Kelby
(German) farm by the spring.

*Kele
(Hopi) sparrow hawk.

*Kel/Kell
(Old Norse) spring.

*Kellagh
(Irish) war.

*Kellen
(Irish) mighty warrior.

Kelton
(English) port; the keel maker's
town.

Kelven/Kelvin
(Irish/English) narrow river.

Kelwin
(Old English/Welsh) friend from
the ridge; white ridge.

Kendrick
(Irish) son of Ken; handsome
son.

*Kenji
(Japanese) second born.

*Kenley
(Old English) the king's meadow.

Kennan
(Scottish) little Ken; little
handsome one.

*Kennedy
(Old English) royal ruler; (Ir)
helmeted chief.

Kenrick
(English/German) handsome,
powerful and hard royal ruler.
A combination of Ken and Rick.

Kent
(Irish) lord; (O/Wel) white;
bright.

Kenton
(Old English) the king's town;
handsome town.

*Keo
(Hawaiian) God will increase.

*Keon
(Irish) young warrior; well born.
A form of Ewan.

Kerem
(Turkish) noble and kind.

Kern
(Irish) infantry leader.

Kerr
(Scandinavian) marsh.

Kerrick
(English) the wealthy king's
estate.

Kers
(Hindi/Native American) plant.

*Kersen
(Indonesian) cherry.

*Kerstan
(Dutch) Christian. A form of
Kirsten.

Kerwin
(Irish/Welsh) dark-haired friend;
dark-complexioned and
fair-haired.

*Kes
(English) falcon.

*Kesse
(Native American/Fanti) chubby baby.

Khal
(Arabic) Friend. A short form of
Khalid or Khalil.

Khalid/Khalil
(Arabic) friend.

Khalif

(Arabic) king.

Khan
(Turkish) prince.

Khristos
(Greek) Christ bearer. A form
of Christopher.

*Kiel
(Irish) from the strait. A form of
Kyle.

*Kiele
(Hawaiian) the gardenia flower;
(Ir) from the strait. A form of
Kyle.

Kieran
(Irish) small and dark-haired.

Killian
(Scottish) small and war-like.

Kingsley
(Old English) the king's meadow.

Kingston
(Old English) the king's town.

Kinnard
(Irish) the king's high hill.

Kioshi
(Japanese) quiet.

Kip
(Old English) pointy hill; a nap.

Kiran
(Sanskrit) light-beam.

*Kirby
(Old English) church by the
farm; cottage near the water.

Kirk
(Old Norse/Scandinavian) church.

Kirkland

(Old Norse/Old English) church
land.

Kirkley
(Old Norse/Old English) church meadow.

Kirkwood
(Old Norse/Old English) church
forest.

Klaus
(German) victory of the people.
A form of Nicholas.

Kline
(German) small.

Knight
(Old English) warrior for the
king.

Knowles
(Old English) grassy sloping
hill.

*Knox
(Irish/Scottish) hill.

Knud
(Danish) kind.

Knute
(Old Danish) relative.

*Ko
(Chinese) change.

*Koby
(Polish/Hebrew) maintainer.
A form of Jacob.

*Kody
(English) cushion.

*Kofi
(Twi) born on a Friday.

*Kohana
(Sioux) fast moving.

Kona

(Hawaiian/Scottish/Irish) ruler
of the world. A form of Don/
Donald.

Konane
(Hawaiian) bright moonlight.

Kono
(Moquelumnan/Miwok) squirrel
eating pine nuts.

Kort
(Scandinavian) wisdom.

*Kory/*Cory
(Irish) hollow; (Ger) helmet.

Kruz
(Spanish/Portuguese) cross.

Kurt
(Latin/German/French)
courteous; enclosure.

*Ky
(Irish/Scottish) strait. A short
form of Kyle.

*Kyan
(Irish) little king from the strait.
A combination of Kyle and Ryan.

*Kyle
(Irish/Scottish) from the strait.

*Kyler
(English/Irish/Scottish) from the
strait. A form of Kyle.

*Kynan
(Welsh) chief.

*Kyne
(Old English) royal; king.

L

Lach/Loch
(Scottish) lake.

Lachlan
(Scottish) land of the lakes.

*Lael
(Hebrew) belonging to the lord.

*Laidley
(Old English) path by the meadow
stream.

Laired
(Scottish) landowner; lord of
the manor.

*Lake
(Latin) pond.

*Lal
(Hindi) beloved.

*Lale
(Latin) lullaby.

Lamar
(German) famous; (Fren) sea.

Lambert
(German) bright and rich estate
owner.

Lamont
(Scandinavian) lawyer; (O/Fren)

mountain.

Lance
(Latin/Old French) the knight's
spear attendant. A short form

of Lancelot.

Lancelot
(Latin/Old French) the knight's
spear attendant.

Landan
(German) open land; (O/Eng) hill
land.

Lander
(English) grassy plain; landowner.

Lando
(Portuguese/Spanish/German)
famous.

Landon
(Old English) grassy landowner;
hill land.

Landric
(German) land ruler.

Landry
(French/English) ruler of the land.

Lane
(Middle English) narrow road;
(Abor) good.

Lang
(Scottish/English) long; (Abor)
tree; (Scand) tall; (Tong) heaven.

Langdon
(Old English) long hill.

Langford
(Old English) long river crossing.

Langley
(Old English) long meadow.

Langston

(Old English) long, narrow town;
Lang's town; town of the tall one.

Lann
(Irish) sword.

Lanz
(Italian/French) knight. A form of
Lance.

Lanzo
(German) land servant.

Lao
(Latin/Spanish) glorious stand;
(Tong) law.

*Lapu
(Hopi) bark of a cedar tree.

*Laris
(Latin) cheerful.

Larkin
(Irish) rough and fierce.

Larnell
(Latin) beloved victory. A
combination of Larry and
Daryl.

Larrimor
(French) armoured.

Larron
(Old French) thief.

Lars
(Latin/Norse) laurel tree; laurel
leaves; victory. A form of
Laurence.

Larson
(Norse) Lars' son; son of victory. A
form of Laurence.

Lateef
(Arabic) gentle.

Latham
(Scandinavian) barn by the

homestead.

Lathan
(Hebrew) gift of God. A form
of Nathan.

Latimer
(Old French) language teacher,
interpreter.

Laughlin
(Irish) servant.

Laurence
(Latin) laurel tree; laurel leaves;

victory.

Lauv
(Latvian/Baltic) lion.

Laval
(Old English) lord.

Lavan
(Hebrew) white.

Lawford
(Old English) low river crossing
by the hill.

Lawler
(Scottish) softly spoken; (O/Eng)
low hill.

Lawley
(Old English) low meadow
by the hill.

Lawrence
(Latin) laurel tree; laurel leaves;
victory.

Lawson
(Latin/Old English) Lawrence's son;
son of victory.

Lawton
(Latin/Old English) Lawrence's
town; town of victory.

Lazaro
(Italian/Greek) resurrection.

Lazarus
(Hebrew) God will help.

Leal
(English) faithful friend.

Leander
(Latin/Greek) lion-like;
faithful.

*Lee/*Leigh
(Old English) meadow; shelter
from the wind; (Ir/Scot) poetic.

Leeland/Leyland
(Old English) shelter; meadow land.

Lei
(Chinese) thunder; (Haw) king;
(Ton) ivory.

Leif
(Scandinavian) beloved;
(Scott/Gae) broad river.

*Leighton
(Old English) meadow town.

Leks
(Estonian) defender of humankind.
A form of Alexander.

Lemar
(French) ocean.

Lenno
(Native American) man.

Lennon
(Scottish) little cap or cloak.

*Lennox
(Scottish) grove of elm trees.

Lenny
(German) brave like a lion. A

short form of names starting
with 'Len' e.g. 'Lennon'.

Leo
(Latin) lion. A short form of
names starting with 'Leo' e.g.
Leopold.

Leon
(French) lion-like.

Leonard/Leonardo
(German) bold and strong like
a lion.

Leonel
(French) lion cub. A form of
Lionel.

*Leor/*Lior
(Hebrew) light of mine.

Lepati
(Tongan) leopard.

Leron
(Old French) circle.

Leroy
(Old French) king.

Lev
(Hebrew) heard. A short form of
names starting with 'Lev' e.g.
Levant.

Levander
(Hebrew) rising from the sea.

Levant
(Latin) rising.

Levi
(Hebrew) united; promise.

Levin
(Old English) dearest friend.

Lewis
(German) famous warrior. A form of Louis.

Lex
(Greek) word; defender of humankind.
A short form of Alexander.

*Li
(Chinese) strength.

Liam
(German) helmet of resolution;
(Ir) wilful. The Irish short form
of William.

*Lian
(Irish) protector.

*Liang
(Chinese) excellent.

Lias
(English) rock.

*Lief
(Old Norse) beloved and praised.

*Linden
(Old English) lime tree valley.

Linton
(Old English) flax town; lime
tree town.

Linus
(Greek) flax; blond-haired.

*Lio
(Hawaiian/French) lion cub.

Lionel
(Old French) young lion, cub.

Liron
(Hebrew) my song.

Lisle
(Old French) island.

Lleyton
(Old English) meadow town.

Loch

(Scottish) lake.

Lochie
(Scottish) land of the lakes. A short
form of Lachlan.

Locke
(Old English) forest enclosure;
(Scot) lake.

Lockwood
(Old English) forest enclosure.

*Logan
(Irish/Scottish) hollow.

*Lok
(Chinese) happy.

*Loki/*Lokie/*Loky
(Old Norse) trickster.

Loman
(Irish) enlightened; (Ir) brave;
(Slav) sensitive.

Lonan
(Zuni) cloud.

Lonato
(Native American) flint stone.

*London
(Old English) long hill. (M/Eng)
fortress of the moon. The capital
of England.

Lono
(Hawaiian) God of farming and peace.

Lorcan
(Irish) little and fierce.

Lorenzo
(Italian/Spanish/ Latin) laurel tree;
laurel leaves; victory. A form
of Lawrence.

Loretto

(Latin/Italian) laurel tree; laurel leaves; victory. A form of Lawrence.

Lorimer
(Old French) saddle, spur and bit maker.

*Loris
(Greek) flowering; (Dut) clown; (Lat) victory; laurel leaves. A masculine form of Chloris/Chloe.

Loritz
(Danish/Latin) laurel tree; laurel leaves; victory. A form of Lawrence.

Lorn/Lorne
(Latin) laurel tree; laurel leaves; victory. A form of Lawrence.

Lothar
(German) war-like.

Loudon
(German) low valley.

Louie/Louis
(German) famous warrior.

*Lourde/*Lorde/
*Lourdes/*Lorde
(French) from Lourdes in France,

holy. A place where the Virgin Mary is believed to have appeared.

*Luc
(Latin) bringer of light; (Heb) rising; light. A masculine form of Lucy and a short form of Lucius.

Lucas
(German/Irish/Danish/ Dutch) bringer of light. A masculine form of Lucy.

*Lucian
(Latin) bringer of light. A

masculine form of Lucy.

Lucius
(Latin) bringer of light. A masculine form of Lucy.

*Lucky
(Middle English) fortunate.

Lucretius
(Latin) gain.

*Luka/Luke
(Latin) light.

*Luken
(Latin/Basque) bringer of light. A masculine form of Lucy.

*Lundy
(Scottish) grove island.

Lunn
(Irish) war-like.

Lyall
(Scottish) loyal.

Lyle
(Old French) island.

*Lyndon
(English) lime tree hill.

*Lyron
(Hebrew/French) circle.

Lysander
(Greek) defender of humankind. A form of Alexander.

Lytton
(Old English) town by the loud stream.

M

*Mabry
(Latin) worthy of love; lovable
beauty; (Ir) joy. A masculine form
of Amabel/Mabel.

Mac/Mack
(Scottish) son.

*Macalla
(Aboriginal) full moon.

Macallister
(Scottish/Irish) Allister's son; son
of the avenger.

Macarthur
(Scottish/Irish) Arthur's son;
son of noble strength; (Wel) bear;
son of the bear.

Macauley
(Scottish) son of righteousness.

Maccoy
(Scottish/Irish) Coy's son; son of
the shy one.

Maccrea
(Scottish/Irish) Grace's son; son
of the graceful one.

Macdonald
(Scottish/Irish) Donald's son; son
of the ruler of the world.

Macdougal
(Scottish) Dougal's son; son of
the dark stranger.

Macharios
(Greek) blessed with happiness.

Mack
(Scottish) son. A short form
of names starting with 'Mack'
e.g. Mackenzie.

*Mackenzie
(Scottish) son of the wise and
beautiful leader.

*Mackinac
(Native American) islands of
turtles.

Mackinley
(Scottish/Irish) Kinley's son; son
from the king's meadow; son from
the family meadow.

Maclean
(Scottish/ Latin/Greek) Leander's
son; son of the lion-like one; son
of the faithful one.

Macmahon
(Scottish/Irish) Mahon's son; son
of the strong bear.

Macnair
(Scottish) Nair's son; son of the heir.

Maco
(Hebrew) God is with us. A
form of Emmanuel.

Macon
(Old English) creating; to perform.

*Maddock/*Maddox
(Welsh) fortunate.

Madeep
(Punjabi) mind that is full
of light.

Maddison/*Madison
(English) son of the powerful
warrior.

Madon
(Irish) charitable.

Magnar
(Norwegian) warrior.

Magnus
(Latin) great.

Maguire
(Irish) Guire's son; son of

the beige one.

Magus
(Latin) wizard; learned.

Mahir
(Hebrew) expert.

Mahon
(Irish) strong bear.

Maidoc
(Welsh) fortunate. A form of
Maddox.

Maka
(Tongan) rock.

Makani
(Hawaiian) wind.

Makis
(Greek/Hebrew) who is like God.
A form of Michael.

Maks
(Hungarian/Latin) great.

Maksim
(Russian/Latin) the greatest.

Makya
(Hopi) eagle hunter.

Mal
(Irish/Scottish) follower of
Saint Columba. A short form

of names starting in 'Mal' e.g.
Malcolm.

*Malach/*Malachi/*Malakai
(French) angel; messenger.

Maldon
(Old English) meeting place in the
forest hollow.

*Malin
(Old English) little warrior.

Malleson
(Hebrew) Mary's son; sea of
bitterness; son of the

lady of the sea.

Malo
(Tongan) thank you.

Malohi
(Tongan) strength.

Malone
(Irish) St John's servant.

Maloney
(Irish) devoted to worship on
Sundays.

*Maloo
(Aboriginal) thunder.

*Mandala/*Mandela
(Yao) flower.

Mandel
(German) almond.

Mander

(Gypsy) myself.

Manhein
(German) servant.

Manning
(Old English) Mann's son; son
of the masculine one.

Mannix
(Irish) monk.

Mansel
(English) the clergy man's house.

Mansfield
(Old English) the man's meadow;
the hero's meadow.

Manton
(Old English) the hero's town; the
man's town.

Manu
(French) man; (Haw/Tong) bird;
(Hind) man; maker of laws;
(Ghan) second born son.

Manuel
(Hebrew/Spanish) God is
with us. The French and Spanish
form of Emmanuel.

Manzo
(Japanese) third born son.

*Marar
(Watamare) dust or mud.

Marc
(Latin) war-like; warrior; (Eng) shining.
A short form of Marcel/Marcus
and a form of Mark.

Marcel/Marcellus
(Latin) war-like; warrior; (Eng)
shining.

Marco
(Latin/Italian) war-like; warrior;

(Eng) shining.

Marcus
(Latin) war-like; warrior;
(Eng) shining.

Marek
(Latin/Slavic) of Mars; warrior.

Marid
(Arabic) rebel.

Mario
(Latin) war-like; warrior; (Eng)
shining; dedicated to the
Virgin Mary. The Italian
form of Mark.

Mark
(Latin) war-like; warrior; (Eng)
shining.

Marlin
(Old English) sea; ocean fish.

Marlon
(Old French) little falcon, hawk.

Marlow
(Old English) hill by the lake.

Maro
(Japanese) myself.

*Marron
(Aboriginal) leaf.

Marsden
(Old English) the warrior's valley.

Marshall
(Old French) horse keeper;
(Amer) law keeper.

Martell
(English) one who hammers.

Martin/Martinus/Marty
(Latin) warrior, war-like.

Mason
(Old French) stone worker.

Massey
(English) twin.

Massimo
(Italian) the greatest. A form of
Max/Maximilian.

*Mata
(Tongan) blade.

*Mato
(Native American) brave; warrior.

Matt/Matthew
(Hebrew) given.

Matu
(Native American) brave; warrior.

Maurice
(Latin/French) dark-haired or
complexioned; marshland.

*Maverick
(English/American) independent;
spirited.

*Max
(Latin) great. A short form of
names starting with 'Max' e.g.
Maxwell/Maxine.

Maxfield
(Latin/English) Mack's field; the
greatest field.

Maximilian
(Latin) the greatest.

Maximus
(Latin) the greatest.

Maxwell
(Old English) the greatest
stream.

Mayer
(Hebrew) light; (O/Ger) dairy worker.

Mckay
(Scottish) Kay's son; pure son.

*Mckenzie/*MacKenzie
(Irish) Kenzie's son; son of the
wise leader.

Medad
(Hebrew) beloved waters.

*Mel
(English/Irish) friend; (Eng) mill;
(Grk/Port/Span) A short form
of names starting with 'Mel'
e.g. Melvin/Melissa.

Meldon
(Old English) mill hill.

Meldrick
(Old English/German) wealthy,
powerful and hard ruler of the mill.
A combination of Mel and Rick/
Richard.

Melvern
(Native American) great chief.

Melville
(Old French/Old English) mill
village.

Mer
(Old English) from the sea.

*Mercer
(Latin) merchant; (Fren) textile
dealer.

Mered
(Hebrew) rebel.

Merrick
(English) ruler of the sea
(Ger/O/Eng) powerful, wealthy
and hard ruler from the sea.

Merrill

(French) famous; (Eng) water.

Meyer
(German) head servant; farmer;
(Heb) bringer of light.

*Micah
(Hebrew) who is here; who is
like God. A form of Michael.

Michael
(Hebrew) who is like God.

Miguel
(Portuguese/Spanish/Hebrew) who
is like God. A short form of Michael.

*Mika
(Omaha/Ponca/Osage) raccoon;
(Heb/Russ) likeness to God. The
Russian form of Michael.

*Miki
(Japanese) tree.

*Milan
(Slavic) beloved.

Miles/Myles
(Latin) warrior; (O/Ger) merciful;
(Eng) distance measurement.

Milford
(Old English) mill by the river
crossing.

Milo
(German) merciful; (Lat) miller.

Milos
(Greek/Slavic) pleasant.

Milton
(Old English) mill town.

*Mingan
(Native American) grey wolf.

*Miron
(Polish) peace.

Miroslav
(Slavic) peace and glory.

Mitch/Mitchell
(Old English) big.

Mitford
(Middle English) big river
crossing.

Montague
(Old French) pointed mountain.

Montaro
(Japanese) big boy.

Monte/Montey/Monty
(Latin) mountain. A short form
of names starting with 'Monte'
e.g. Montega/Montego.

*Montega
(Native American) new arrow.

Montez
(Spanish) mountain.

Montgomery
(Old French) wealthy mountain. .

Monti
(Aboriginal) stork.

Montre
(French) show.

*Montreal
(French) royal mountain.

Monty
(English) wealthy mountain. A
short form of names starting
with 'Mont' e.g. Montgomery.

Moore
(Old French) dark-complexioned;
(O/Eng) marshland.

Morel
(French) mushroom.

Moreland
(English) marshland.

Morey
(English/Greek) dark-
complexioned; marshland.
A short form of Morris.

Morio
(Japanese) forest.

Morland/Morley
(Old English) marsh meadow;
dark meadow.

Morrell
(Old French) dark-haired or
complexioned.

Morris
(Latin) dark-haired or
complexioned; marshland.

Morrison/Morse
(Latin/Old English) son of Morris;
dark-haired or complexioned son;
son from the marshland.

Mort
(Middle English) stump. A short
form of names starting with 'Mort'
e.g. Mortimer.

Morten
(Latin/Norwegian) warrior; war-like.
A form of Martin.

Mortimer
(Old French) still waters; (Ir) sea
director.

Morton
(Old English) marsh town.

Morven
(Scottish) sea mariner; (Celt) sea
raven; (Ir) dark-haired or

complexioned.

Moses
(Hebrew) drawn forth; (Egypt)
child.

Moswen
(African) fair complexioned.

Moulton
(Old English) town with mules.

*Mozart
(Italian) breathless.

Muir
(Scottish) marsh.

Mundy
(Irish) from Reamonn, Ireland.

Mungo
(Irish) lovable.

*Muraco
(Native American) white moon.

Murphy
(Irish) from the sea.

Murray
(Scottish) sailor from the
settlement.

Mustafa
(Arabic) royal; chosen.

*Myall
(Aboriginal) drooping acacia.

Myer
(Hebrew) light.

Myers
(English) swamp owner.

Mykal
(Hebrew) who is like God. A
short form of Michael.

Myles
(Latin) warrior; (O/Ger) merciful;
(Eng) distance measurement. A

form of Miles.

Myron
(Greek) fragrance.

N

Naal
(Irish) birth.

Nabil
(Arabic) noble prince.

*Nacoma
(Comanche) wanderer.

Nadav
(Hebrew) generous and noble.

Nadim
(Arabic) friend.

Nadir
(Arabic/Afghani) rare and dear.

*Nahele
(Hawaiian) forest.

Naim
(Arabic) happy.

*Nain
(Aboriginal) lookout.

Nair
(Old English) heir.

*Nairn
(Irish) one who can't swim; (Scot) alder tree river.

Naite
(Tongan) knight.

Najib
(Arabic) born into nobility.

Nakos
(Arapaho) wisdom; the sage herb.

Naljor
(Tibetan) holy.

*Namid
(Chippewa) star dancer.

Namir
(Arabic) swift like a leopard.

Narain
(Hindi) guardian.

*Narn
(Aboriginal) sea.

Narrie
(Aboriginal) bushfire.

*Nash/*Nashville
(Old English) northern ash tree; northern ash tree village; from Nashville; adventurous.

*Nat
(Hebrew/English) gift of God. A short form of Nathan/Nathanial.

*Natal
(Latin) birth; born at Christmas time. The Spanish form of Noel.

*Natane
(Polynesian) gift.

Nate
(Hebrew) little gift. A short form of
Nathan/Nathaniel.

Nathan
(Hebrew) gift. A short form of
Nathaniel.

Nathanial/Nathaniel
(Hebrew) gift.

*Nattai
(Aboriginal) water.

*Navarro
(Spanish) plains.

Naveed
(Hindi) bringer of good thoughts.

Navin
(Hindi) new.

Neco
(Egyptian) lame.

Ned
(English) wealthy guardian. A short
form of Edward.

Nels
(Scandinavian/English) Neil's son;
son of the champion. A short form
of Nelson.

Nelson
(English) Neil's son; son of the
champion.

Nen
(Egyptian) ancient water.

Neo
(Greek) new; (Tswana) gift.

Nevan
(Irish) holy.

Newell
(Old English) new spring.

*Nic/Nicho/Nico/*Niko
(Greek) victory of the people. A
form of Nicholas.

Nicholas
(Greek) victory of the people.

Nicholson
(Greek/English) Nicholas' son; son
of the victorious people.

*Nic/Nick/*Nicky
(Greek) victory of the people. A
short form of Nicholas.

Nien
(Vietnamese) year.

Nigan
(Native American) ahead.

Nika
(Yoruba) brutal.

Niles
(English) Neil's son; son of the
champion.

Nino
(Spanish) young child.

Nixon
(Old English) Nicholas' son; son
of the victory.

Noah
(Hebrew) long rest; peace.

*Nocona
(Comanche) one who wanders.
A form of Nacoma.

*Noe
(Hebrew/Spanish) peace.

Noel
(Latin/French) born at Christmas

time.

*Nolan
(Irish/Scottish) descended from
nobility; famous.

Norbert
(Scandinavian) bright hero.

Noris/Noriss
(Old French) northerner.

Northcliff
(Old English) northern cliff.

Northrop
(Old English) northern farm.

Norton
(Old English) northern town.

Norville
(Old English) northern village.

Norwell
(Old English) northern stream.

Norwood
(Old English) northern forest.

Nowles
(English) grassy slope.

Numair
(Arabic) panther.

Numid
(Native American) star dancer.

Nye
(Old English) islander.

O

O'Connor
(Irish) high desire.

Oak/Oake/Oakes/Oakey
(Old English) oak trees.

*Oakley
(Old English) oak tree meadow.

Obadiah
(Hebrew) servant of God.

Oberon
(French) obedient; king of the
fairies.

Oberyn
(French) obedient little king.
A combination of Oberon and
Ryan.

Obie
(English) servant of God. A short
form of Obadiah.

Ocan

(Luo) hard times.

Odam
(Middle English) son-in-law.

*Odell
(Scandinavian) wealthy; little;
(O/Eng) valley.

Oden/Odin
(Scandinavian) ruler.

Odon
(Hungarian) wealthy protector.

Odran
(Irish) pale green colour.

Ogden
(Old English) valley of oak trees.

Oisin
(Irish) small deer.

Oke
(Hawaiian/Scandinavian) divine
spearer; (Tong) oak tree. A form
of Oscar.

Oko
(Yoruba) God of war.

Olaf
(Old Norse) heirlooms.

Olando
(Italian) famous land.

Oleg
(Latvian/Russian) holy.

Olin
(English) holly.

Oliver/Ollie
(Latin/Old French) olive tree;
(Scand) holy. A masculine form
of Olivia.

Omar
(Arabic) first born son; follower

of the prophet.

*Omari
(Swahili/Arabic) highest follower
of the prophet. A form of Omar.

*Ona
(Latin/Scottish) unity; (Lith)
graceful; (Grk) donkey.

*Onan
(Turkish) prosperous.

O'Neil
(Irish) Neil's son; son of the
champion.

*Oren
(Hebrew) pine tree; (Gae)
pale-complexioned.

Orford
(Old English) upper river
crossing.

*Ori
(Hebrew) light.

*Orien
(Latin) visitor from the east.

*Orin
(Irish) white.

Orion
(Greek) son of fire; son of light.

Orlan
(English) pointed land.

*Orlando
(German) famous land.

Oron
(Hebrew) light.

Orrick
(English) old oak tree.

Orrin
(English) river.

Orson
(Latin) bear.

Orville
(Old French) golden village;
(Eng) oval-shaped village.

Orvin
(English) friend with a spear.

Oscar
(Old English/Scandinavian)
divine spearer.

O'Shea
(Irish) Shea's son; son of the
majestic one; son from the
fairy palace.

Osmar
(Old English) divinely glorious.

Osric
(English) divine ruler.

*Ossian
(Irish) fawn.

Osten
(Latin) held in high regard.

Oswin
(Old English/Welsh) divine
friend; divine and fair-haired.

Othello
(German/Spanish) wealthy.

Otis
(German/Old English) son of
Otto; son of the wealthy one;
(Grk) keen of hearing.

Otto
(German) wealthy.

Owen
(Welsh) well-born.

Owney
(Irish) elderly.

Oxford
(Old English) river crossing
for oxen.

Oxley
(Old English) meadow of the oxen.

P

Pablo
(Latin/Spanish) small. The
Spanish form of Paul.

Paco
(Native American) bald eagle;
(Ital) pack.

Paddy
(Irish) noble. An Irish short
form of Patrick.

Padre
(Spanish) priest.

Palben
(Basque) blonde-haired.

*Palladin/*Pallaton
(Native American) warrior.

*Palmiro
(Greek/Latin) land where palm
trees grow; born on Palm Sunday,
the Sunday before Easter. A
masculine form of Palmira.

Pancho
(Spanish/English) honest; from
West Germany, (Lat) freedom;
from France. A form of
Frank/Franklin.

Park/Parker
(Middle English) common or garden
area; guardian of the park; (Chin)
cypress tree. A short form of Parker.

Parkin
(English) little Peter; little rock.

Parlan
(Scottish) farmer; (Eng) park land.

Parnell
(Latin/Old French) little Peter;
little rock.

*Parri
(Aboriginal) stream.

Parrish
(English) district of the church.

Parry
(Welsh) Harry's son; son of the
army ruler; (Eng) to ward off an
attack.

*Pas
(Latin) dance.

*Pascal
(Italian) born at Easter time.

*Pastel
(English) drawing; light colours.

*Pat
(Latin/Irish) little and noble. A
short form of names beginning
with 'Pat' e.g. Patrick/Patricia.

Patrick
(Latin/Irish) noble.

Patterson

(Latin/Irish) Pat's son; son of
nobility.

Pax/Paxton
(Latin) peace town.

Payne
(Latin) pagan; country person;
civilian. A form of Pagan.

Paytah
(Lakota) fire.

Paz
(Latin/Spanish) peaceful.

Peadar
(Irish) small rock. A form of
Peter.

Pearson
(Scottish) Peter's son; son
of the rock.

Peder
(Latin/Scandinavian) small rock.
A form of Peter.

Pembroke
(Irish/Welsh) headland; hill;
stream.

Pendle
(Old English) hill; enclosure on
the hill.

Penley
(English) enclosed meadow.

Perez
(Hebrew) to break through.

Perry
(Old English/Greek) rock. A
form of Peter and the short form
of Peregrine.

Peter
(Latin) rock.

Petyr
(Latin) rock.

Phelan
(Irish) wolf; fierce.

Phelps
(English) Philip's son; son of the one
who loves horses.

Philander
(Greek) lover of humankind.
A combination of Philip and

Alexander.

Philip
(Greek) one who loves horses.

*Phoenix
(Greek) immortal.

Piao
(Chinese) handsome.

Pierce
(English) sharp.

*Pinon
(Native American) stars.

*Pinto
(Native American) horse with
white patches.

Porter
(Latin) gate keeper; (Eng)
luggage carrier.

Pradeep
(Hindi) light.

Prasad
(Hindi) brilliant.

Prentice
(Middle English) apprentice.

Prescott
(Old English) the priest's cottage.

*Preslee/*Presleigh/*Presley
(Old English) the priest's meadow.

Preston
(Old English) the priest's town.

Primo
(Italian) first born.

Q

Qadir
(Arabic) powerful.

Qamar
(Arabic) moon.

Qasim
(Arabic) divider.

Qing Nan
(Chinese) young.

Quab
(Vietnamese) allowed.

*Quabin
(Aboriginal) quality lake.

*Quain
(French) clever.

*Quamby
(Aboriginal) restful; shelter.

*Quan/*Quana
(Comanche) fragrant.

*Quaringa
(Aboriginal) island.

*Quay
(English) wharf.

*Quennel
(Old French) little oak tree.

*Quentin
(Latin) fifth born.

*Quenton
(English) the queen's town.

*Quigley
(Scottish) flax meadow; (Ir) maternal.

*Quillan
(Irish) cub; youngster.

*Quiller
(Old English) writer.

*Quillon
(Latin) sword.

*Quimby
(Norse/Old English) from the queen's village.

*Quincy
(Latin/Old French) the fifth son's estate.

*Quinlan
(Irish) strong, athletic; (Eng) the queen's land.

*Quinn
(Irish/Scottish) the advisor's descendant; (Eng) queen.

Quinto/Quiqui
(Spanish/German) ruler of the house. A form of Henry.

*Quirin
(English) magic spell.

*Quiver
(English) arrow holder.

*Quon
(Chinese) bright.

R

*Radlee/*Radleigh/*Radley
(Old English) red meadow.

Radolf
(Old English) fast wolf; fierce
advisor.

Rafael
(Hebrew/Spanish) God has
healed. A form of Raphael.

Rafferty
(Irish/Scottish) prosperous
and rich; on of prosperity.

Raghnall
(Irish) powerful wisdom; strong.

Ragnar
(Norwegian/Swedish) mighty army.

*Rainer
(Old German) warrior of
judgment; advisor.

Raja
(Hindi) king; ruler.

*Rajah
(Aboriginal) stars.

Ralph
(Old Norse) wolf advisor;
fierce advisor.

Ralston
(Old English) Ralph's town; town
of the wolf advisor or fierce advisor.

Ramiro
(Portuguese/Spanish) supreme
judge.

Ramsay
(Old English) ram or raven island;
wild garlic island.

Ramsden
(Old English) ram's valley.

Ranan
(Hebrew) fresh luxury.

Rance
(African) borrowed; (Fren) marble.

Rand
(English) warrior.

Randall/Randolph/
Randie/Randy
(Old English) shielded wolf who
protects; fierce protector.

Ranen
(Hebrew) joyful singer.

*Rangi
(Māori) sky.

Ranier
(English) great army.

Rankin

(Old English) little shield; little protector.

Ranon
(Hebrew) joy.

Ransford
(Old English) the raven's river crossing.

*Ranslee/*Ransleigh/
*Ransley
(Old English) the raven's meadow.

Raphael
(Hebrew) God has healed.

Rashad
(Arabic) wise advisor.

Rashid
(Arabic) giver of directions.

Rashidi
(Swahili) sound advice.

Rasmus
(Greek) loved.

Ratan
(Hindi) gem.

Rauf
(Arabic) kindhearted.

Raul
(Old Norse) wolf advisor; fierce advisor. A form of Ralph.

Raulas
(Latin/Lithuanian) laurel tree; laurel leaves; victory. A form of Lawrence.

Rav/Ravi
(Hindi) sun.

Ravid/Raviv
(Hebrew) rain; dew; adorned with

jewels.

Rawdon
(Old English) rough hill; roe deer hill.

Rawlee/Rawleigh/Rawley/
Rawly
(English) roe deer meadow.

Rawlins/Rawson
(Old English) son of the little wolf; son of the little and fierce advisor.

Raydon
(Old English) rye hill; stream by the hill.

Rayfield
(Old English) stream meadow; rye meadow.

Rayford
(Old English) stream river crossing; rye river crossing.

Rayhan
(Arabic) favoured by God.

Raynor
(Scandinavian) mighty army.

Razi
(Aramaic) secret.

*Reade
(Old English) red-haired.

*Reagan/*Regan
(Irish) little king; royal.

*Red
(English/Australian) red-haired.

Redford
(Old English) red river crossing; reedy river crossing.

Redlee/Redleigh/Redley

(Old English) red meadow.

*Reece
(Welsh) enthusiastic.

Reed
(Old English) red-haired;
water grass.

Reeve
(Middle English) steward.

Regan
(Irish) little king; royal.

Regin
(Scandinavian) judge.

Regis
(Latin) king-like.

Rei
(Japanese) law.

Reid
(English) red-haired; reed, water
grass.

Reidar
(Norwegian) warrior of the nest.

Reinhart
(German/French) wise, bold
and courageous.

*Remi/*Remy
(French/English) raven; from
the champagne town Rheims.
A short form of names starting
with 'Rem' e.g. Remington.

Remigius/Remus
(Latin) fast.

Remington
(Old English) the raven's town.

Renald/Renaldo
(Spanish/English) advisor of
the king; powerful; and mighty. A

form of Reynold.

Renato
(Italian) reborn; (Heb) song of joy.
A masculine form of Renata.

Renaud
(French) powerful.

Rendor
(Hungarian) police officer.

*Renny
(Irish) prosperous; small and strong.
A short form of names starting with

'Ren' e.g. Renato/Renee.

Renshaw
(Old English) the raven's forest.

Renton
(Old English) roe deer town.

Renzo
(Latin) laurel tree; laurel leaves;
victory. A short form of Lorenzo.

Reuben
(Hebrew) son.

Rex
(Latin) king.

Rexford
(Old English) the king's river
crossing.

Rexton
(Old English) the king's town.

Rey
(Spanish) king. A form of Ray.

Reyhan
(Arabic) favoured by God.

Rhett
(English) mighty; (Wel) ardent;
red; enthusiastic; (Grk) well
spoken; pearl; mighty.

*Rhidian
(Welsh) river crossing.

*Rhodes
(Greek) roses.

Rhydwyn
(Welsh) white river crossing.

Rhys
(Old Welsh) ardent.

*Rian
(Irish) little king. A form of Ryan.

Ricardo
(Old German/Portuguese/
Spanish/English)
powerful and wealthy ruler.
A form of Richard.

Richard
(Old German) wealthy, powerful
and hard ruler.

Richmond
(Old French/Old English) powerful
and hard mountain; (O/Ger)
powerful protector.

Rick/*Ricky
(German) wealthy, powerful
and hard ruler. A short form
of Richard/Rickard.

Rickard
(Swedish/German) wealthy,
powerful and hard ruler.
A form of Richard.

Ricker
(English) powerful army.

Rico
(Spanish) ruler of the home. The
Spanish form of Henry.

Rickon
(German/English) wealthy,
powerful and hard ruler.

Riddock
(Old English) smooth field.

Rider/Ryder
(Old English) horse rider.

Ridge
(Old English) from the ridge.

Ridgley
(Old English) ridge meadow.

*Ridlee/*Ridleigh/*Ridley
(Old English) red meadow.

Riel
(Hebrew/Spanish) strength
of God. A short form of Gabriel.

Rigg
(Old English) ridge.

*Rilee/*Rileigh/*Riley/
*Ryley
(Irish/Scottish) valiant; war-like;
courageous; (O/Eng) rye meadow.

*Riordan
(Irish/Scottish) royal poet.

Rip
(Dutch) full grown; ripe. A short
form of Ripley.

*Riplee/*Ripleigh/*Ripley
(Old English) the shouter's meadow;
strip of wood in the clearing.

*Rive
(French) river.

*River
(Latin/French/English) large stream.

*Roan
(Old English) rowan tree.

Roarke
(Irish/Scottish) famous ruler.

Robb/Robby/Robbie
(Old German/Old English) bright
and famous. A short form of
Robert.

Robert
(Old German/Old English) bright
and famous.

Robertson
(Old German/Old English) Robert's
son; son of the bright and famous one.

*Robin/*Robyn
(Old English) the robin bird;
bright and famous; (O/Eng)

bright flame. A form of Roberta
and a feminine form of Robert.

Robinson
(Old English) Robin's son; son
of the robin bird; son of the
famous and brilliant one; son
of the bright flame.

Rocco
(Italian) rock.

Roch
(Old German) peace and
tranquillity.

Rochester
(Old English) stone camp.

Rock
(Old English) stone.

Rockford
(Old English) stone river
crossing.

Rocklee/Rockleigh/
Rockley/Rockly
(Old English) rocky meadow.

Rockwell
(Old English) rocky stream.

Rocky

(Old English) rock. A short
form of Rockwell.

Rodden
(Old English) roe deer valley.

Rogan
(Irish/Scottish) red-haired.

Rogelio
(Spanish) famous warrior.

Roger
(Old German) renowned
spearer.

Rohan
(Hindi) sandal wood; (Eng) rowan
tree.

Roland
(Old German) famous land.

Roman
(Latin) from Rome, Italy.

*Romany
(Gypsy) wanderer, gypsy; (Lat)
from Rome, Italy.

Romeo
(Italian) pilgrim of Rome.

*Romney
(Welsh) curving river.

*Romy
(Latin/Italian) from Rome. A short
form of names starting with 'Rom'
e.g. Roman.

Ronan
(Irish) little seal; promise.

*Rondel
(French) short poem.

Ronson
(Old English) Ron's son; son of
the mighty and powerful one.

Roone
(Old English) mysterious, magic sign; (O/Eng) advise.

Rooney
(Irish/Scottish) red-haired.

Roose
(Old Dutch) rose; (Fren) red-haired.

*Rory
(Lat) aurora; dawn; Ir) red-haired royal; king.

Roscoe
(Scandinavian) deer forest.

Roshe
(Hebrew) chief.

Rosmer
(Danish) sea horse.

Rouke
(Irish) mighty.

*Rousse
(French) red-haired.

Rove/Rover
(Middle English) wanderer; (Eng) dog.

*Rowan
(Scandinavian) red berry tree; (Scot) rowan tree; (Eng) famous friend; (Ir) little red-haired one; (O/Nrs) mountain ash tree.

Rowell
(Old English) roe deer stream.

Rowland
(Old English) rough land; roe deer land.

*Rowlee/*Rowleigh/ *Rowley
(Old English) rough wood clearing;

roe deer meadow.

Rowson
(Irish) Row's son; son of the red-haired one.

Roydon
(Old English) rye hill; the king's hill.

Royston
(Old English) town by a stone cross.

Rozario
(Latin) rosary.

Rozen
(Hebrew) leader.

Ruadhan
(Irish) little red-haired one.

Rudolph
(Old German) famous wolf; fierce.

Rudy
(Old English) red-haired.

Rudyard
(Old English) red enclosure.

Ruford
(Old English) red river crossing.

Rufus
(Latin) red-haired.

Rupert
(Italian/English) famous and brilliant. The Italian form of Robert.

Rurik
(Scandinavian) famous king.

Rush
(French) red-haired; (Eng) reeds.

Rushford

(English) reedy river crossing.

Russ
(Old French) little red-haired one;
fox. A short form of Russell.

Russell
(Old French) red-haired; fox.

*Rusty
(Old French/English) red-haired.

Rutherford
(Old English) castle river
crossing.

Rutland
(Old Norse) stump.

Rutlee/Rutleigh/Rutley
(Old English) stumpy meadow;
red meadow.

*Ryan
(Irish/Scottish) little king;
royal.

*Ryder/*Rider
(English) rider of horses.

Ryderson
(Old English) Ryder's son;
son of the horse rider.

Rylan
(Old English) rye land.

Ryle
(Old English) rye hill; rye island.

Ryne
(Irish) little king; royal. A form of Ryan.

S

Saad
(Arabic) lucky.

Saber
(French) sword.

*Sacha
(Greek) defender of humankind.
A short form of Alexander.

*Sage
(Latin) healthy; wise; herb.

*Sahale
(Native American) falcon.

*Sahen
(Native American) falcon;
(Hind) above.

Sahir
(Arabic/Hindi) friend.

Sahn
(Vietnamese) comparing.

*Sal
(Italian) saved. A short form
of Salvatore.

Salid
(Arabic) lucky.

Salvadore
(Italian) saved.

*Sam/*Sammy
(Arabic) praised; (Heb) asked of
God; heard of God. A short form
of names starting with 'Sam'

e.g. Samantha and Samuel.

*Sami
(Hebrew) highly praised. A native
people of Norway, Sweden, Finland
and Russia.

Samir
(Arabic) entertaining.

Samson
(Hebrew) his son; his ministry;
sun-like.

Samuel
(Hebrew) his name is God; heard of
God; asked of God.

Samwell
(Hebrew/Old English) stream asked
of God; stream heard of God. A form
of Samuel.

Sanborn
(English/Scottish) sandy stream.

Sancho
(Spanish) saintly; holy and pure.

Sandeep
(Punjabi) enlightened.

Sanders

(Greek) Alexander's son; son of
the defender of humankind.

Sanditon
(Old English) sandy town.

Sandler
(Hebrew) shoemaker.

Sandor
(Greek/Hungarian/Slavic) defender
of humankind. A form of Alexander.

Sanford
(Old English) sandy river crossing.

*Sani
(Navajo) elder; (Hindi) the

planet Saturn.

Sanjay
(Sanskrit) conscience.

*Santana
(Spanish) saint.

Santiago
(Spanish) Saint James; God's
gracious saint.

Santo
(Spanish/Italian) saint.

Santon
(Old English) sandy town.

Saul
(Hebrew) borrowed.

Sauts
(Cheyenne) bat.

*Saville
(French) willow tree village;
from Saville; prophet; (Fren)
willow tree town.

Sawney
(Scottish) protector.

Sawyer
(English) one who works with
a saw.

Sawyl
(Welsh) child who was asked for.

Saxby
(Old Norse) farm with the
short sword; near the Saxon
town.

Saxon
(Old English) a Saxon.

Sayed
(Arabic) prince.

Sayers
(Welsh) carpenter.

Scanlon
(Irish) little scandal.

*Schuyler
(Dutch) shield; scholar.

Scott
(Old English) from Scotland.

*Scully
(Irish) town crier.

*Seain
(Irish/Hebrew) God is gracious.
A form of Sean.

Seamus
(Irish) God is gracious. A form
of Sean/Shane.

*Sean
(Irish) God is gracious. A form
of Shane/Shawn.

Seanan
(Irish) old and wise.

Sebastian
(Latin) honoured above all

others.

Sedgley
(Old English) sword-shaped
meadow.

Sedgwick
(Old English) sword-shaped
grass.

Seeley
(Old English) blessed meadow;
meadow by the sea.

Sef
(Egyptian) yesterday.

Sefton
(Old Norse/Old English) town
in the rushes.

Seif
(Arabic) religion's sword.

*Sein
(Basque) innocent.

*Selby
(English) farmstead.

Selwin
(English/Welsh) blessed,
fair-haired friend.

*Sen
(Japanese) wood fairy.

Senan
(Irish) old.

Senson
(Spanish) live.

*Seoirse
(Irish) farmer. A form of
George.

*Serafino
(Spanish/Italian) the highest

order of the angels; (Heb) beloved.
A masculine form of Seraphina.

Serge
(French) moving forward.

Sersa
(Illyrian) worthy of reverence;
king.

Seth
(Hebrew) appointed; set.

Seton
(Old English) sea town.

*Shae/*Shai/*Shay/
*Shaye

(Hebrew) gift; (Ir) fairy palace.
A masculine form of
Shay/Shaye.

Shamus
(Irish) God is gracious. A
form of Sean/Shane.

Shanahan
(Irish) wisdom.

*Shane/*Shayne
(Irish) God is gracious.

*Shanlee/*Shanleigh/
*Shanley
(Irish) child of the hero;
(Heb/Eng) God's gracious
meadow.

*Shannon
(Irish) small, wise; slow stream.

*Shappa
(Sioux) red thunder.

*Shaun/*Shaughn/
*Shawn
(Irish) God is gracious. A
form of John/Shane/Sean.

Sheary/Sheehan

(Irish) peaceful.

*Sheldon
(Old English) hill by the sea;
ledge.

Shelpey
(Old English) sheller of peas.

Shelton
(Old English) beachside town.

Shep
(Old English) sheep. A short
form of names starting with
'Shep' e.g. Shepley.

Shepherd
(Old English) sheep herder.

Shepley
(Old English) sheep meadow.

Shipley
(Old English) sheep meadow;
(Eng) meadow by the shipping
port.

Shipton
(Old English) sheep town; (Eng)
ship town.

Shiva
(Hindi) life and death.

Sid
(Old French) from St Denis; (Eng)
wide; (Phoe) enchanter. A short
form of Sidney.

Silvan
(Latin) from the forest.

Silvester
(Latin) from the forest.

Simon
(Hebrew) hearing; obeying.

*Sion
(Hebrew) highly praised.

*Sivan
(Hebrew) born during the
ninth month of the Jewish year.

Skene
(Scottish) bush.

Skerry
(Norwegian) stone island.

Slade/Sladen
(English) muddy valley.

Slane
(Slavic) salty.

Slavin
(Irish) mountain man;

mountain climber.

*Sloan/*Sloane
(Scottish/Irish) warrior.

*Sohan
(Hindi) charming.

*Sol
(Spanish/Norse/Latin) sun.

Soloman
(Hebrew) peace.

Solon
(Greek) wisdom; grave.

Son
(Native American) star; (Viet)
mountain; (Eng) son.

Songan
(Native American) strength.

Sonny
(Old English) son; (Nat/Amer)
star; (Russ) wisdom. A short
form of names ending in 'son'
e.g: Jackson and a Russian
masculine form of Sophie.

Sono
(Akan) elephant.

Soren
(Danish) thunder; war.

*Sorley
(Old Norse) Viking; summer
wanderer.

Spencer
(English) dispenser of
provisions.

Spiro
(Latin) breath of God.

Stafford
(Old English) staff-shaped river
crossing.

Stamford
(Old English) stone river
crossing.

Stamos
(Greek) crown. A form of
Stephen.

Stanley
(Old English) stone meadow.

Stannis
(Slavic) glorious stand. A
short form of Stanislaus.

Stanton
(Old English) stone town.

Stanway
(Old English) stone path; road.

Stanwick
(Old English) stone village.

Stanwood
(Old English) stone forest.

Stark
(German) strength; bare.

Stavros
(Greek) crowned. A form of
Stephen/Steven.

Steele
(Old English) steel worker.

Steenie
(Scottish) crowned. A form
of Stephen.

Stefan
(Polish/Russian/Swedish/Swiss)
crowned. A form of Stephen.

Stein
(Norwegian/German) stone.

Steinar
(Norwegian) stone warrior.

Stephen
(Greek) crowned.

Stephenson
(Greek/English) Stephen's son;
son of the crowned one.

Sterling
(English) silver; silver penny.

Stern
(German) star; (Eng) hard.

Steve/*Stevie
(Greek/Australian/Dutch/
New Zealand/English) crowned.
A short form of Steven/Stephen.

Steven
(Greek/Australian/Dutch/
New Zealand/English) crowned.
form of Stephen.

Stig
(Old Norse/Swedish) rising;
mount.

Stinson
(English) Stone's son; son of
the stone one.

Stockley
(Old English) farm animals in
the meadow.

Stoker
(English) tender of the furnace.

Stone
(Old English) stone.

*Storm/*Stormie/
*Stormy
(Old English) tempest.

Storr
(Old Norse) great.

Stover
(English) tender of the kiln; cook.

Stowe
(Old English) place.

Strahan
(Irish/Scottish) poet; wisdom.

Stratford
(Old English) street by the river
crossing; street by the river valley.

Stratton
(Scottish) river valley town; main
street in the town.

Sullivan
(Irish/Scottish) black eyes.

*Sully
(Old English) dark meadow;
southern meadow.

*Sumner
(English) summoner.

*Sun
(Chinese) bend; (Eng) sun.

Sundeep
(Punjabi) enlightened.

Sven
(Norse) youthful.

Svenbjorn
(Norse) young bear.

Swain
(English) attendant of the
knight.

Swaley
(English) winding stream in
the meadow.

Sweeney
(Irish/Scottish) little hero;
(O/Eng) strength.

*Sydney/*Sidney
(Old French) from St Denis;

(Eng) wide; (Phoe) enchanter.

Syed
(Arabic) happy.

T

Ta
(Chinese) great.

Tadashi
(Japanese) serves faithfully.

Tadd
(Old Welsh) father.

Tahir
(Arabic) pure.

*Tai
(Chinese) kin; weather; talented.

*Tailor/*Taylor
(Old English) tailor; maker or
repairer of clothes. A form
of Taylor.

*Tain/*Tayne
(Scottish) stream.

*Tainn
(Native American) new moon.

Tait
(Old Norse) happy.

*Taj
(Hindi) crown.

*Takeo
(Japanese) strength.

*Takota
(Sioux) friend to everyone.
A form of Dakota.

*Tal
(English) tall; (Heb) rain; dew.

Talbot
(German) commander; valley;
(Fren) cobbler, boot maker.

Talcott
(Old English) tall cottage.

*Tale
(Tswana) green; (Eng) story
teller.

Talman
(Aramaic) harsh; (Eng) tall man.

*Tamar
(Hebrew) palm tree; date fruit.
A masculine form of Tamara.

*Tamas
(Hebrew/Hungarian) twin; (Hind)
night. A form of Thomas.

*Tamir
(Arabic) palm tree.

Tamson
(Hebrew/English/Scandinavian)
son of Thomas; son of the twin.

Tane
(Māori) husband.

*Taniel
(Hebrew/Estonian) (Hebrew)
God is my judge; gift of God.
A form of Danielle or Daniel
and a feminine short form of
Nathaniel.

Tanne
(Greek/Lettish) priceless. A form
of Anthony/Tony.

Tanner
(Old English) leather worker.

Tanton
(Old English) quiet and still river

near the town.

Tarleton
(Old English) thunder town;
Thor's town.

*Tarn/*Tarne
(Old Norse) mountain pool.

*Taron
(Greek/English) the king's
courageous advisor.

Tarrance
(Latin/English) smooth, good
and gracious. A form of Terence.

Tarrant
(Welsh) thunder.

Tarver
(Old English) softener of whitened
hide; tower over the hill.

*Tas

(Gypsy) bird nest.

*Tate
(Old English) cheerful;
(Native Amer) long talker;
(O/Eng) spirited; cheerful.

Taved
(Estonian) beloved. A form
of David.

Tavey
(Latin) eighth born; beloved.
A short form of Octavio and
the Scottish form of David.

Tavi
(Aramaic) good.

Tavis
(Hebrew/Scottish) David's son;
son of the beloved; (Aram) good.

Tavish
(Scottish) twin. A form of Thomas.

*Taylor/*Tailor
(Old English) tailor; maker
and repairer of clothes. A
form of Tailor.

Taz
(Persian) goblet.

Teague
(Native American) low rider;
(Eng) handsome; (Ir) poet.

*Teal/*Teale
(Middle English) sea green/
blue; duck.

Tearlach
(Scottish) strong and courageous.
A form of Charles.

Tearle
(English) stern.

Teman

(Hebrew) right; south.

*Tennyson
(Old French) Tennant's son;
son of the house renter.

*Teo/Tayo
(Spanish) gift of God.

Tevis
(Scottish) twin. A form of
Thomas.

Tex/Texas
(Native American) friendly;
(USA) from Texas, U.S.A.

Thane
(English) attending warrior.

Thaniel
(Hebrew) gift. A form of
Nathaniel.

Theo
(German) prince of the people.
A short form of names starting
with 'Theo' e.g. Theodore.

Theodore
(Greek) gift of God.

Theon
(Greek) hunter; (German) prince
of the people.

Theron
(Greek) hunter.

Thian
(Vietnamese) smooth.

Tho
(Vietnamese) longevity.

Thom
(Hebrew/English) twin. A short
form of Thomas and a form
of Tom.

Thomas

(Hebrew/Aramaic) twin.

Thompson
(Hebrew/English) Thomas' son;
son of the twin.

Thor
(Scandinavian) thunder; God
of thunder; (O/Nrs)
strong thunder.

Thorald
(Scandinavian) Thor ruler;
thunder ruler.

Thorburn
(Scandinavian) Thor's bear;
thunder bear.

Thorleif
(Scandinavian) Thor's beloved,
beloved thunder.

Thorley
(Old English) thorny meadow;
(Scand/O/Eng) Thor's meadow;
thunder meadow.

Thormond
(Scandinavian/Old English)
under Thor's protection;
thunder protection.

Thorn/Thorne
(Old English) prickle, thorn.

Thornley
(Old English) thorny meadow.

Thornton
(Old English) thorny town.

Thorpe
(English) village farmstead.

Tiarnach
(Irish) devout.

*Tiba

(Navajo) grey.

*Tien
(Chinese) heaven.

Tiennan
(French) crowned; (Ir) master. A
form of Stephen/Steven.

Tierney
(Irish) royal; lordly.

Tilon
(Hebrew) hill.

Tim/Timmy
(Greek) honouring God. A short
form of Timothy.

Timin
(Arabic) born near the sea.

Timo
(Finnish) honoured by God. A

short form of Timothy.

Timothy
(Greek) honouring God.

Timur
(Hebrew) stately; (Russ)
conqueror.

Tirril
(Wemba-Wemba) sky.

Titus
(Greek) giant.

Tivon
(Hebrew) lover of nature.

Tobi
(Yoruba) great.

Tobias
(Hebrew) God is good.

Toby
(Hebrew) God is good. The short

form of Tobias.

Todd
(Latin/Middle English/Norse) fox.

*Tohon
(Native American) cougar.

Tom/Tommy
(Hebrew/Aramaic/ English) twin.
A short form of Thomas.

Toma
(Tongan) show off.

Tomer
(Hebrew) tall.

Tomkin
(Hebrew/Aramaic/Old English)
little Tom; little twin.

Tomlin
(Hebrew/Aramaic/English) little

Tom; little twin from the pool.

Tommen
(Hebrew) twin.

Tor
(Irish) rock; (Nor) thunder;
(Tiv) king.

Torbert
(Old English) bright and rocky
hilltop.

Torger
(Scandinavian) Thor's spear;
thunder spear.

Torin
(Irish/Scottish) chief.

Tormod
(Scottish) northerner.

Tormund
(Scottish/English) northern
mountain; (Scand/O/Eng) under

Thor's protection; thunder protection.

Torr
(Old English) tower; rocky peak;
(Scand) Thor; thunder.

Torrance
(Irish/Scottish) small and rocky hill.

Torrant
(Latin) tender.

Torrent
(English) fast and rocky stream.

Torsten
(Scandinavian) Thor's stone; thunder stone.

*Tory/*Tori
(Scandinavian) Thor; thunder;
(Jap) bird; (Lat) victory.
A masculine form of Tori/
Victoria.

Toshiro
(Japanese) intelligent and talented; sincerity.

Tove
(Scandinavian) Thor's rules; thunder rules.

Tovi
(Hebrew) good.

Trai
(Vietnamese) pearl.

Travers
(French) crossroads.

Travis
(Old French) keeper of the crossroads or tax collector.

Trent
(English) cunning; (Lat) fast

moving stream; (Fren) thirty.

Trenton
(Latin/English) town by the fast-moving stream.

Trevelyan
(Scottish) Elian's homestead; the uplifting one's homestead.

Trey
(Middle English) third born; three.

Trigg
(Old Norse) trustworthy.

Tristan/Tristram
(Old Welsh) loud; bold knight;
(Fren) sorrowful.

Troy
(Irish/Scottish) son of the foot soldier; (Fren) curly-haired;
(Eng) water.

Tuan
(Aboriginal) spear; (Viet) unimportant.

Tui
(Māori) handsome songbird;
(Tong) faith.

*Tully
(Irish/Scottish) one who lives with the peace of God; mighty people.

*Tuyen
(Vietnamese) angel.

Twain
(English) rope maker.

Ty/Tye
(English) enclosure. A short form of names beginning with 'Ti' or 'Ty' e.g. Tyler.

*Tyee
(Native American) chief.

Tyler
(Old English) maker or layer of tiles.

Tynan
(Irish/Scottish) dark-haired.

Tyr
(Norse) born of war.

*Tyree
(Scottish) island dweller.

Tyrion
(Norse/Irish) Little king born of war.

U

Udell
(Old English) valley of the yew trees.

Ulan
(African) first born of twins.

Ulfer
(Norse) warrior wolf; fierce warrior.

Ull
(Norse) magnificent will.

Ulmer
(Old Norse) fierce wolf; fierce and famous.

Ulric/Ulrich/Ulrick
(Old German) hard and noble ruler; fierce; wolf ruler; supreme ruler; (O/Nrs) reward; (Ir) mind; (Dan) wolf; fierce.

Ultan
(German) noble stone; (Ir) trouble stone.

Umar
(Arabic) blooming.

*Umi
(Malawian) life.

Upton
(Old English) estate in the upper town.

Ure/Uri/Uriah
(Hebrew) light of God.

Ursan/Ursel/Ursus/
Ursine
(Latin) bear. A masculine form of Ursula.

Urvil
(Hindi) sea.

Usama
(Arabic) lion.

Useni
(Malawian) telling.

Usenko
(Russian) son of the man with the moustache.

Usher
(English) one who seats others.

*Usi
(Malawian) smoke.

Uzi
(Hebrew) strength.

Uziah
(Hebrew) God is my strength.

Uziel
(Hebrew) strength.

Uzoma
(Nigerian) born while traveling.

V

*Vaal
(Dutch) valley.

Vachel
(Old French) one who raises
small cows.

*Vada
(Latin) shallow water.

Vaha
(Tongan) open sea.

*Vail
(Old English) valley.

*Val
(Latin) strength; (Eng) valley. A
short form of names starting
with 'Val' e.g. Valentine.

*Vale
(Old French) valley.

*Valentine/Valentino
(Latin) strength. A masculine
form of Valentina.

Valerian
(Latin) strength.

Valgard
(Norse) foreign spearer.

*Vali
(Tongan) paint.

*Valin
(Hindi) mighty warrior.

*Vallis
(Old French) from Wales.

Valmiki
(Hindi) ant hill.

Valu
(Polynesian) eighth born.

Vamana
(Sanskrit) one who deserves
praise.

Van
(Dutch) born of nobility;
belonging to or from.

Vance
(Middle English) very high
place; swamp.

Vander
(Dutch) belonging to or from.

Vane

(Dutch/German) belonging
to or from.

Varad
(Hungarian) fortress.

Varden
(Old French) green hills.

Varen
(Hindi) better.

Varesh
(Hindi) God is better.

Varian
(Latin) intelligent.

Varick
(Icelandic) drifting on the sea.

Varil
(Hindi) water.

Varun
(Hindi) water God.

*Varuna
(Russian) one who sees all.

Vasil
(Slavic) king. A form of Basil.

Vasilis
(Greek) magnificent knight;
warrior.

Vaughan
(Irish) small.

Vaux
(Old French) valley.

Veiko
(Finnish) brother.

Veit
(German/Swedish) wide.

Venn
(Irish/Scottish) fair-haired;
(Eng) marshland.

*Vere
(Latin) faithful; (Swed) sacred
wisdom; (O/Ger) defender. A
masculine form of Verena.

*Vered
(Hebrew) rose.

*Verlin
(Latin) flourishing, blooming.

*Vic
(Latin) victory. A short from of
Victor/Victoria.

Victor
(Latin) victory. A masculine form
of Victoria.

Vincent
(Latin) conqueror.

Vlas
(Russian) one who stammers.

Volkan
(Turkish) volcano.

W

Wade
(English) dweller in the water;
advance.

Wagner
(Dutch) maker of wagons.

*Wai
(Māori) water.

Waine
(English) wagon driver.

Waite
(Middle English) guardian.

Wakely

(Old English) damp meadow;
white meadow.

Walden
(English) valley in the forest.

Waleed
(Arabic) newborn.

Wallace/Wallis
(English) from Wales; stranger.

Walt
(German) powerful warrior. A short
form of names starting with 'Walt'
e.g. Walter.

Ward
(Old English) guardian.

Warden
(Old English) guardian of valley.

Warick
(Old English) hero of the village.

Warner
(German) protecting warrior.

Warwick
(Old English) house by the
dam; the warrior's homestead.

Wentworth
(Old English) white homestead
or farm.

Wes
(English) west. A short form of
names starting with 'Wes' e.g.
Wesley.

Weston
(Old English) western town.

Whalley
(English) hill meadow.

Whittlee/Whitleigh/
Whitley

(English) white meadow.

Wickham
(Old English) enclosure in
the village; (Eng) fenced
farmhouse.

Wickley
(English) meadow in the village;
wicker meadow.

Wies
(German) famous warrior.

Wilbur
(German) bright and wilful.

Wilder
(English) from the wilderness.

Wiley
(English) willow tree meadow.

Wilhelm
(German) wilful. A form of
William.

Wilkinson
(Old English) little William's son;
son of the Wilful one.

Will/Willie/Willy
(Old English) Wilful. A short
form of names starting with
'Wil' e.g. William.

Willard
(German) Wilful and brave.

William
(German/Old English) Wilful.

Williams
(German/Old English) William's
son, son of the Wilful one.

Willis
(German/Old English) William's
son; son of the Wilful one.

Wilson
(German/Old English) William's
son; son of the Wilful one.

Wilstan
(German) wolf stone; fierce
stone; (O/Eng) Wilful stone.

Wilton
(German/Old English) Will's
town; the Wilful one's town.

Windsor
(German) river bend.

Winfield
(Old English/Welsh) the
friend's meadow; white
meadow; (Eng) windy meadow.

Wolf/Wolfe
(German/English) fierce; wolf.

Wolfgang
(German) fierce leader; (Eng)
leader of the wolf pack.

Wolfram
(German) wolf raven; fierce raven.

Wyatt
(Middle English) Guy's son; son
of the guide; (Eng) white; (Fren)
little warrior; (Amer) wide.

Wyck/Wick
(Scandinavian) village.

X

Xenos
(Greek) stranger.

Xevadiah
(Hebrew) God will give.

Xeven
(Slavic) lively; (Eng) seven;
seventh born.

Xi Wang
(Chinese) desire.

*Ximen/*Ximenes
(Hebrew/Spanish) hearing;
obeying. A form of Simon.

Ximran
(Hebrew) sacred.

Xindel

(Hebrew) protector of humankind.

Xing Fu
(Chinese) happy.

Xion
(Hebrew) guarded land.

Xiu Mei
(Chinese) plum.

Xowie
(Greek) life. A masculine
form of Zoe.

Xylon
(Greek) forest.

Xan/Xander
(Greek) defender of humankind.
A short form of Alexander.

Xaver
(Spanish) bright.

Xavier
(Arabic) bright; owner of the
new house. The masculine
form of Xaviera.

Xayvion
(Arabic) new home.

*Xen
(Japanese) spiritual;
(Chin) pure.

Y

*Yael
(Hebrew) mountain goat.

Yakim
(Hebrew) God develops.

Yakir
(Hebrew) honoured beloved.

Yale
(Welsh/Old English) elder.

Yamal
(Hindi) twin.

Yamin
(Hebrew) son of the right
hand; favourite. A form of
Benjamin.

Yancy
(Native American) Englishman.

Yardan
(Arabic) king.

*Yardley
(Old English) enclosed
meadow.

Yarin
(Hebrew) understanding.

Yarran
(Aboriginal) acacia tree.

*Yas
(Navajo) snow.

Yasar
(Arabic) wealthy.

Yashar
(Hebrew) honourable.

Yates
(English) gate keeper.

Yavin
(Hebrew) God is
understanding.

Yazid
(Arabic) growing.

Ye
(Chinese) universe.

Yen
(Chinese) desire;
(Viet) calm.

Yeoman
(Middle English) long time
servant of the family.

Yered

(Hebrew) coming down.

Yeriel
(Hebrew) found by God.

Yerik
(Russian) God has praised.

Yestin
(Welsh) just. A form of
Justin.

Yevgeny
(Greek/Russian) noble and
wellborn; God is gracious. A
masculine form of
Eugenie and a form of Eugene.

Yigael
(Hebrew) God will redeem.

Yitzhak
(Hebrew) happy.

Yo
(Chinese) bright.

Yona
(Native American) large
bear.

Yong
(Chinese) brave.

Yonus/Yonah
(Arabic/Hebrew) dove. A
form of Jonah.

Yora
(Hebrew) teacher.

Yorick
(English) farmer.

York
(Irish) yew tree farm.

Yosef
(Hebrew) God has added

a child; increasing; perfect. A
form of Joseph.

Yosha
(Hebrew) wisdom.

*Yoshi
(Japanese) quiet.

*Yotimo
(Native American) bee flying
into its hive.

Yuan
(Chinese) original.

Yudan
(Hebrew) judgment.

Yukiko
(Japanese) snow.

Yukio
(Japanese) snow boy.

Yul
(Chinese) over the horizon.

Yule
(Old English) born at
Christmas time.

Yuma
(Native American) son of
the chief.

Yusuf
(Hebrew/Arabic) God has

added a child; increasing; perfect.
A form of Joseph.

Yutu
(Native American) coyote hunting.

Yvan
(Russian) God is gracious. A
form of Ivan.

Yves

(French) knight of the lion;
archer's bow. The masculine
form of Yvette and Yvonne.

Ywain
(Greek/Welsh) well born.

Z

Zac/Zack
(Hebrew) God remembers.
A short form of names starting
with 'Zac' e.g. Zachary.

Zaccheus
(Hebrew) pure.

Zacharia/Zachariah
(Hebrew) God remembers.

Zachary/Zackary
(Hebrew) God remembers.

Zacker
(Hebrew/Bavarian) God
remembers. A form of Zachary.

Zafar
(Arabic) winner.

*Zahar
(Hebrew) dawn.

Zahavi
(Hebrew) gold.

Zahid
(Arabic) self-denying,
abstinent.

Zahir
(Arabic) apparent and
understood.

Zahur
(Swahili) flower.

Zaid
(Arabic) increasing.

Zaim
(Arabic) general.

Zaine
(English) God is gracious. A

form of Zane.

Zak/Zaki
(Arabic) smart; (Heb) God
remembers. A form of Zachary.

Zako
(Hebrew/Illyrian) God has
remembered. A form of
Zachary.

Zakur
(Hebrew) masculine.

Zale
(Greek) power of the sea.

Zales
(English) salt.

Zalman
(Hebrew) peace. A form

of Solomon.

Zalmir
(Hebrew) songbird.

Zamiel
(German) God has heard.

Zamir
(Hebrew) song.

Zan
(Hebrew) well fed.

Zander
(Greek) defender of humankind.
A form of Alexander.

Zane
(English) God is gracious.
The English form of Shane/
John.

Zareb
(African) guardian.

Zared
(Hebrew) ambush.

Zarek
(Slavic) God will protect.

Zattu
(Hebrew) beautiful.

Zavad/Zavao
(Hebrew) present time.

Zavier
(Bohemian) bright.

Zayd/Zayn
(Arabic) handsome.

Zayvion
(African American) new
homeowner.

Zeal
(Latin) energy.

Zebadia/Zebadiah
(Hebrew) God's gift.

Zebedee
(Greek) my gift.

Zebulon
(Hebrew) dwelling place;
honourable.

Zeev
(Hebrew) wolf.

Zehariah
(Hebrew) God's light.

Zeheb
(Turkish) gold.

Zeira
(Aramaic) small.

Zeke
(Arabic) intelligent.

Zeki
(Turkish) smart.

Zelig
(Jewish) holy and blessed.

Zelimir
(Slavic) peace is desired.

*Zemariah
(Hebrew) song.

*Zen
(Japanese) spiritual; (Chin) pure.

*Zenas
(Greek) living; welcomed. A masculine
form of Xena/Zena.

*Zenda
(Slavic) well born.

Zenith
(Latin) highest point.

*Zeno
(Greek) sign; living; welcomed;
from Zeno. A masculine form
of Zena/Xena.

Zenobias
(Greek) given life by Zeus.

*Zephaniah
(Hebrew) protected and treasured
by God.

Zephyrus
(Hebrew) wind from the west.

Zerach
(Hebrew) light.

*Zerah
(Hebrew) brightness of
the morning.

Zerem
(Hebrew) stream.

*Zerika
(Hebrew) rainstorm.

Zesiro
(Nigerian) first born of twins.

Zethan
(Hebrew) shining.

Zethus
(Greek) son of Zeus; king of
the Gods; living; bright sky. A
form of Zeus.

Zeus
(Greek) living; bright sky.

Zev
(Hebrew) living; wolf; fierce.

Zevach
(Hebrew) sacrifice.

Zevariah
(Hebrew) God has given.

*Zevi
(Hebrew) deer.

Zevid
(Hebrew) present.

Zeviel
(Hebrew) gazelle of God.

Zhong
(Chinese) second brother.

Zhu
(Chinese) wish.

Zhuang
(Chinese) strength.

Zif
(Hebrew) wolf.

*Ziggy
(German) victorious protector.
A short form of Sigmund.

Zilpah
(Hebrew) trickling.

Zimen
(Hebrew/Spanish) hearing;
obedient. A form of Simon.

Zimraan
(Arabic) celebrated.

Zimri
(Hebrew) valuable.

Zinan
(Japanese) second born son.

Zindel
(Hebrew) protector of
humankind.

Zinon
(Greek) living.

Zion

(Hebrew) sign.

Zissi
(German) freedom.

Ziv
(Hebrew) bright with life.

Zivan
(Hebrew) bright.

Ziven
(Slavic) lively.

Ziya
(Arabic) light.

Ziyad
(Arabic) increasing.

Zohar
(Hebrew) bright.

*Zola
(German) prince.

Zoltan
(Arabic) sultan; great ruler.

Zoltin
(Hungarian) life.

Zomeir
(Hebrew) tree pruner.

Zomelis
(Lithuanian) asked of God.

Zonar
(Latin) sound.

Zoro
(Persian) star.

*Zorya
(Slavic) star.

*Zowie
(Greek) life. A masculine
form of Zoe.

Zsolt
(Polish) ruler.

Zuberi
(Swahili) strength.

Zubin
(Hebrew) praised highly.

Zuriel
(Hebrew) God is my stone
foundation.

Zwi
(Scandinavian) gazelle.

Zygfryd
(Polish) glorious peace. A form
of Siegfried.

Zylon
(Greek) forest dweller.

Zymon
(Hebrew) hearing; obeying. A form
of Simon.

Printed in Great Britain
by Amazon